RISING
FROM THE
RUBBLE

RISING
FROM THE
RUBBLE

A TRUE STORY BY
WILLIAMSON SINTYL

ARISE
PROJECT FOR HUMANITY

Rising from the Rubble

Copyright © 2022 Williamson Sintyl

Published by:
Williamson Sintyl

For information contact:
ariseprojects.org
ikoneklifecoaching.com
Or email support@ariseprojects.org

Book cover design: Stacey Gold Macey
Interior book design: Francine Platt · EdenGraphics.net

ISBN: 978-1-63972-990-6

Printed in the United States of America

DEDICATION

*To the coming generations, this book is a
reminder of all the wonderful journeys upon us.
May it invite us to rise from our circumstances,
and the rubble of our own lives.*

*To my eternal wife and best friend
Sharla Kjar Sintyl and my precious children
Tevin, Kai, Sidonie . . .*

My family, friends, and supporters!

And my country, Haiti.

This book is a combined effort of my team, who has stood by me throughout the entire process to help bring this venture to life. I'm so grateful to my supporters, for inspiring and motivating me to share my personal story so that more hearts may be touched and hear the invitation to rise and be somebody. I'm grateful for my ancestors, whom I believe are so proud of this work, and my mission on earth to empower others to rise!

WHY I WROTE THIS BOOK

THIS BOOK is about my personal story of surviving the 2010 earthquake in Haiti, and how I rose from the rubble of that disaster as a stronger, more resilient person with renewed vigor and purpose in life. *Rising from the Rubble* will give youth, adults and emerging leaders everywhere a road-map for digging out from under their own metaphorical rubble —whatever that load or burden may be—to become the person they are meant to be. My hope is that all who read this book can find a means of cultivating more purpose, meaning, and service to others in their own lives in a wholesome, helpful, and inspirational way.

CONTENTS

INTRODUCTION

In 2010, I was buried under a three-story building after it collapsed. For twenty-eight grueling hours, I was trapped without food or water, breathing in stale air. There are numerous books about near-death experiences, but this is not one of those books. I knew I would live. I knew I would see the sunshine on my mother's face and enjoy fresh air again. Rather than just write about the story of survival, I wanted to also write about what comes next.

WHAT COMES NEXT after everything literally comes crashing down around you? How do you face the destruction and devastation that come from severe life-altering experiences? When there are struggles in life, and you don't know where to go, where do you turn?

We all have moments that devastate us in some way, whether it is physically, mentally, emotionally, or spiritually. How do we find the fortitude and strength to lift ourselves off our knees, wipe off the dust, and rise from the rubble?

This is about the destruction around me as an earthquake shattered my home and my country. This is about the strength that my people showed in the days, weeks, even years following the devastation. More than that, this is about the strength that we each need to continue to build as we move towards our purpose. This is about the strength that each of us can find and cultivate when faced with dismay, destruction, and devastation.

In this book, I share personal stories from my life. Not only do I share the experiences surrounding the earthquake, but also those events that prepared me to rise from the rubble, just as you are being prepared every moment of your life.

There are many stories of opportunities I have gratefully received since those days; to show you how you can recognize your own strengths, merits, advantages, and opportunities. Further included are also things that have motivated me to keep going and rise from the rubble every time I am faced with a new challenge.

I fully know that I have a mission to complete and a purpose for living through that experience when so many I knew and loved around me did not survive. This is not just a story of physical survival. We are meant to do and to be more than just survivors. We are destined to be magnificent people. We each have a mission and a purpose to our lives.

There is a far grander picture that we sometimes don't entirely appreciate when we get caught up in the little inconveniences of every day. For me, my purpose was made clear when I was trapped by the earthquake. Unable to move, I was given a great gift under that building. I was given time to think about things that were really most important. I was given an opportunity to make a promise to God.

That experience has helped me to make much better choices and create a better life. As I share these experiences, I know that your experiences will be different, more varied, and distinct. However, the principles applied will be the same. Our choices and promises we make change us. Our intentions and actions change the world around us. When we follow through with these wise choices and promises, big things do happen. Like ripples from a rock skipping across a pond, the biggest changes can come from the smallest of choices.

These small daily choices we make create the fabric of the reality we live. The promises we make to ourselves, and others, depend on following through with tenacity and conviction to the end. These choices and promises can be used to our benefit, or can be used to cause harm towards ourselves and others. This book provides some ways your different choices empower you to give and receive the best that life has to offer. You are capable of great things.

The choices that I made have taken me to

amazing places. I am so grateful for the blessings I have received from my experiences. I want to share those blessings with you. I want for you to live a life that will bring you greater purpose, excitement, gratitude, and fulfillment. I know that there are steps we must each take to do this. I want to share my story with you so you can see those steps. Each step will bring greater blessings, even when things become difficult. Each step helps us to rise from our own rubble, rebuild, and move forward with greater clarity.

We live in a world that is full of the very best life has to offer. However, we get distracted, trapped, overloaded, and buried under it all. Rising from the rubble doesn't happen overnight. It only took twenty-eight hours to be freed from the building that had me trapped. However, it sometimes takes years for us to see progress on our journey.

Each and every day since, I have moved towards where I am now. Every hour I continue to take steps to move forward. I know I will fulfill my mission because I live it every day. Just like I knew each minute I would live by choosing to stay awake, by choosing to take another breath, and most importantly, by making promises to God that would allow me to receive all of His blessings.

As you take the time to read this book, also take the time for yourself to think about your own mission and purpose. Again, it may take time, but each step allows the path to become clearer and clearer. It may be a struggle, but you can also pull yourself and your purpose out from your own rubble that keeps you trapped.

Each breath I took under that building was one step closer to surviving, yet it was each breath after that I am grateful for, because they are each a blessing. Every breath you take is important. It is part of the precious gift of life.

We find our greatest conviction in the fight and the struggle. Maybe you don't have to struggle with physical breath, but your conviction will come as you fight to uncover the precious purpose buried inside you. Your conviction will continue as you live and strengthen that purpose daily.

Think of how much you could accomplish if you start today, or even now. You started something by reading my book. You are already taking the right steps. Keep reading for the next steps to take.

ONE

THE DREAMS ON MY SHOULDERS

I dedicate this chapter to my twenty five classmates and every single soul that didn't survive the 2010 earthquake in Haiti. Over 200,000 humans left their dreams hanging in suspense here on earth because of that earthquake. I feel like on that fatal day in Haiti so many dreams and aspirations were placed in the atmosphere to be scooped up, one by one. One dream at a time, we can make them come true, if we just believe that we can. So many sacrifices are made while living in a country like Haiti. I want to honor those sacrifices for those that died, and those that live. I want to fulfill their dreams. Most of all, I want their love for the country to be glorified. Before, when I thought of a dream, I thought of it as a cloud floating lightly in the sky. Now, after emerging from clouds of dust, concrete, stone, blood, and all that tried to shatter me, I can honestly say that dreams aren't so light and fluffy to me anymore. They are big, strong, and powerful shards of emotion, empathy, and determination that I've been destined to carry on my shoulders. I am proud to be the dream-keeper of the soulmates that now lead me to keep pushing.

N 2010, the earthquake in Haiti struck just before 5 pm, just two hours after my mom picked me up from my school. The tremor was felt as far away as Cuba and Venezuela, but the epicenter of the 7.0-magnitude quake was just 16 miles away from Port-au-Prince, the capital, where I lived. I was barely able to get to my parent's orphanage when the building started shaking.

The building collapsed during the first big shake. There were 12 of us under that three-story building. A little boy named TiBlanc was next to me and 11 other children under 14 years old were a few feet away from where I was. Guerline, Samdi, Tiklè, Roberto, Pepe, Roody, Darline, Sonson, Midi, Jenny and Midline. These kids had been living in the orphanage for over 5 years.

It was my job to help my parents by entertaining them and making sure they all had eaten something. The orphans were able to go visit their family every summer. Many orphans in Haiti have parents, but the parents send them to an orphanage if they can't take care of them. When the building fell the only thing I was able to do was to grab TiBlanc who was closest to me and put him under me. Under that rubble it was so hard to breathe, I felt compressed, my back was heavy with a big wall on top of me. I was basically in the child's pose, crouched over the top of TiBlanc, arms over my head and kneeling on my knees.

We all were screaming for the first while, hopeful that maybe someone would come. "Anmwey!!! Vin edem!!!" or "Hello!! Come help me!!!" My dad was out in the street when the earthquake happened so I was hopeful he was looking for me. The aftershocks continued to happen every 5 seconds while I was under the building and the big wall that fell on my back was getting heavier and I couldn't move.

The other kids next to me were suffering and I could hear them trying so hard to call for me but they couldn't. They were too small to carry these heavy blocks and walls on their shoulders. After an hour or so, I started throwing up because there was no circulation in my body and all of the vomit dried to my face. I couldn't even move a finger or arm to wipe it off.

During our mortal life here on earth we will all carry dreams on our shoulders. As honorable human beings it's our duty to remember not to carry those dreams as burdens, but as a responsibility. It is our responsibility to recognize that our soul's dreams are really what God has written to be our purpose. Our responsibility is our privilege to serve others and make the world around us a little bit better.

At some point we start to realize our dreams are about more than just ourselves. Those dreams become bigger than us. There are many stories in this book that have been in my heart and on my shoulders for years. Some of them are stories I have never told anyone.

Growing up, I was very different from those around me. I was the only kid in my entire neighborhood that never drank, partied, or got into mischief. I never did anything out of turn that I shouldn't. I always felt that I needed to protect myself by doing all the right things and by working hard. I've always felt God's hands over me. I knew, even if that knowing was subconscious, that I had a greater calling.

This book is about being vulnerable and bearing my soul to all of you. The dreams and visions you choose to fulfill in this life, will not only abundantly serve you, but most importantly, will change the lives of those rising behind you.

There will come a moment in your life when a tiny light bulb in your head will go off. It does not matter if that light bulb ignites when you are in your 20's or in your 50's, the significance is its presence and the knowing that it is your sign as a call to action.

In that moment you cannot sit and wait for magic to happen. It doesn't work that way. God moves through us all, but we have to show Him our movements. We have to put in hard work and energy, so that the same energy is returned to us in the form of rewards and blessings.

Not everyone will understand that your dream is not just your dream. You don't own that dream, it belongs to the generations behind you and the ones in front of you that are also doing all they can to help those dreams become a reality. I have received support from both those who have come before and those in the future I am working for.

I reach down deep to pull my power for those that are weakened by despair, those that need to draw hope from the strength of my convictions. We are meant to be leaders to the light. By carrying your dreams on your shoulders it will take you to a place of rising above anything. That is my dream for all of you.

I've been set apart to stand my ground for my people in Haiti. The weight that still sits on my shoulders is that my people will lose hope. I don't want them to lose sight of hope for Haiti. Though it seems that Haiti is getting worse everyday, I know it will rise from the ashes.

One of my biggest dreams was to come to America and succeed—to make it!—so that I could expand on the resources needed to give back to my people. While I was under that building, I started imagining myself not being able to live this dream anymore because I couldn't see a way for us to make it out. You see, that is the very type of mind chatter that traps us inside the matrix of uncertainty.

Those are actions of the flesh. We must understand that we aren't in control. We don't have to know every detail of our next steps. God doesn't expect us to figure it all out by ourselves, because he's already done the work. He's already mapped it out. The blueprint is written. We just have to make the move to show Him that we will obey. This is how we find the keys to unlock the doors and keep moving forward. A vision always begins with a tiny spark of hope.

My hope has always been to ignite the tiny spark into flames, bursting into an inferno of pride, for achieving what seemed like the impossible so many times. Sometimes when we can't tangibly see our hopes and dreams, we sink into the anxiety of self destruction.

I want to be that tangible thing for all of you. I want to fuel your ambition. Today, I can honestly say that I am the dream for so many. I am the walking, talking, touchable, lovable, foresight of the dream. At some point in life we have to adjust our perception of why we're here. We have to gain clarity as to our true purpose and how it will touch the lives of others through dreams attained.

All of these thoughts, feelings, and emotions swarmed me while I lay there still helplessly under the rubble. What would my next hope be, what would I think up next to keep myself and TiBlanc alive and breathing, how would I keep a tear from falling so that my little friend that was under me would stay strong? What would be the reason for me to keep going?

Finding Purpose and Direction

Sitting under the rubble, I asked myself so many questions, and found many answers. What did I want to be? Why were my dreams more important than anyone else's? There must be a reason.

My heart broke when I heard, after escaping the rubble, that all 25 of my classmates that stayed to do their homework died. These were my best friends, how would I live without them? As the months passed, all these thoughts and memories merged into a solid resolve: it was now my responsibility to carry their dreams on my shoulders.

When I was finally able to go see what was left of the school, it broke my heart into pieces all over again. I could imagine them, each of them, as they were the last time I'd seen them, whole and alive, laughing and joking, studying and learning.

I cried and poured out my heart to God, telling him that I remembered the promise I made to him. That I wouldn't forget it. That

I wouldn't waste this opportunity that I had been given. My classmates couldn't be here to make the world a better place, to make their country a better place, but I could. I had lived. And it must be so that their legacies could live on through me. I wouldn't let them down.

I understand now that this was my first experience recognizing what was sacrificed for me. My classmates sacrificed their earthly lives so that I could experience the emotion I needed, to pull not only myself out of the rubble, but our country as well. Their pain, last breaths, and suffering was and is meant to fuel my passion of unifying my country.

I now understand that my classmates' physical bodies are no more, but they are a part of my invisible army. Honestly, who doesn't need one of those? That's what we must remember, our ancestors, and loved ones do not die in vain, they continue on, by paving the way for the greater good. They continue on for you and for me. I understand now that asking why I was chosen to live isn't the right question anymore.

TWO

PREPARING THE PATH

You are all special and have been given proper power to be here and your path has been made only for you. Remember no matter how hard the path seems to be, you just keep trudging forward. Even slow, heavy steps are better than no steps. Keep striving at your very best to cross over and carry out your dreams, You are not alone. There's a point in our lives when we will go into a deep introspection. We will have to dive deep and reflect on the moments when we listened to our gut feeling, when we learned to become attuned to our intuition. Trusting ourselves becomes the main tool to surviving on the path. In preparation for the journey you will realize that meditation and prayer become an intricate part to elevating us to a higher level of guidance and wisdom. We have to structure the mind to set a plan that will beat the odds. We have to prepare a path that will lead us

to our destination. While we are on that path, we become warriors, pillars of light, and the protectors of our own destiny.

EIGHT AFTERSHOCKS followed that night while I was under the building with the kids in the orphanage. I felt every one of those shocks. Every tremor made it feel like the building was collapsing down harder on me. It was so heavy, that my right arm was being crushed. My arm was literally giving in to the weight of the stone and rubble. My bones were breaking while I lay there, clenching my teeth, gasping for air, and praying for God to give me the strength to stay awake. In the moments that I was fighting for my life, fighting for the independence to walk out on my own two feet, fighting for the disaster to be over, I started questioning myself. Why? Why was I going through this?

I felt at that moment I was grasping for the breath of every citizen in Haiti. If I didn't get out, they wouldn't get out, WE wouldn't EVER get out. If I was stuck under the rubble, Haiti would forever be stuck grasping, clawing, scratching for air. Lifeless. "NO. I have to get out of here. NOW. My country needs me."

Each of us has been prepared to travel the path we are on. I believe that Haiti influenced many great things to come into the world. In 1791, Haitian slaves began a revolution. The slave uprising led to Haiti's independence from France and the abolition of slavery in the new nation.

Haiti's fight for independence was physical, but it prepared Haitians to receive spiritual and emotional freedom. The history of the island prepared the people of today for a better Haiti.

Haiti's earliest struggles began when France gave up its power in 1791. France was considered a power house of its time, and had built an empire of new lands in America during this period. France honed in on profitable growth by means of coffee and sugar. Sugar dominated the trade markets throughout Haiti (which back then was called St. Domingue.) Haiti had become one of the greatest sugar capitals of the world. A little less than half of Britain and France's sugar was made in Haiti, as was a little more than half of its coffee. ALL of this vast and profitable gain was turned through the hands of slaves.

During that time there was nearly a dozen black slaves to one white person. Slaves in

Haiti were treated less than humanely, and often died of viral infections. These infections were brought on by the harsh living conditions in which the people were forced to survive. There was such a high turnover of the people enslaved. Slave suffrage passed on from generation to generation through a strict structure determined at birth. A mark that couldn't be hidden in society.

While the miserable treatment of slaves in Haiti went on, there remained hope and determination from the blacks that were free. They were inspired by quality in all that they had learned from republican liberals. In 1790, France gave them the right to vote. However, St. Domingue's (Haiti) government refused to recognize this law. This in turn was the beginning of a revolution that would strike out in violence, corruption, and rebellion. A civil war had begun.

Slaves brutally murdered their masters and took down the plantations they had once worked. A violent uproar had inflamed through the country of Haiti. Determined and relentless, slaves fought to change their fate. Finally, the fight to end their suffering won the attention of the french government enough for them to eradicate slavery. Haitian general, Francio Dominique Toussaint Louverture, a revolutionary and prominent leader of his time, led the slaves into dominating the island of Hispaniola, St. Domingue (Haiti), and Santo Domingo.

During this time Napoleon Bonaparte had a dream of his own. He coudn't stand the thought of the new land being taken over by slaves. He felt that his aspirations of having a french domain in America would be undone if slaves took over it. He didn't care that they were now free, having honorably fought their way out of bondage.

He looked down upon the whole ordeal and devised a plan to take the island back and enslave them all over again. His plan did not succeed. When Bonaparte's army forced their way in to seize Haiti, the the revolting slaves refused to move. They stood their ground against the brutal attack.

Bonaparte began to realize that his dreams of using what is now New Orleans as a trade market for products, produced in Haiti, may be null and void. Then United States president, Thomas Jefferson, was mortified at the idea of such violence coming so close to

America. Jefferson used the quandary to American advantage. He offered to purchase New Orleans.

This was significant to American trade and Jefferson fretted about the French owning it. Notably, France sold the whole state of Louisiana to the American country.

Just as Haiti fought to prepare its path to freedom, now I will decide to prepare my next footsteps for the next generations.

Our history is part of our identity, whether we choose it or not. The experiences of our ancestors influence the life we live today. It affects the choices we continue to make every day, even if that choice is to no longer follow things our parents have taught us.

It isn't just our family history that influences and prepares our path. It is also the country where we live. Growing up in Haiti was a very different experience than that of someone who grew up in the United States, France, or the Dominican Republic. Each country has a different history that prepares our path by influencing the people around us and the belief systems we hold.

The history of our country affects the culture we grow up in. Even the language we speak prepares our minds to accept or reject certain ideas and ways of thinking. The mission of each individual is unique, so each journey is different. Every journey follows a path. That path is divinely guided along the way so we can fulfill our unique purpose.

We each have a vital role to play, even if we don't see it. Many American history books don't show the role of Haiti in the Louisiana Purchase or the American Revolution, but it was vital nonetheless. Likewise, our roles extend far beyond what we can comprehend. Stretching from before our earliest memory and reaching far beyond our life on this earth, we have to remember to keep the bigger picture in mind.

It is so easy to get caught up in the little day-to-day inconveniences and irritants. When we can remember how we have been prepared in the past and see our larger role for the future, we can focus on what really matters.

Sometimes we are being prepared for other things. Things that we would never have imagined would be possible. Sometimes the preparation is to receive. What we receive is not always something physical that has been handed to us. Often, what we receive is an opportunity. Each opportunity we are given is a gift. We must go forward into these opportunities and use them.

Opportunities

Have you ever given something to someone who didn't want the gift? If you repeatedly try to offer gifts and they repeatedly refuse, you are less likely to continue trying to give them a gift. The same happens with opportunities. If we do not accept them, we will receive fewer and fewer. Use it or lose it. This choice to use it or not allows people to climb or sink under the rubble of our lives. Seizing opportunities helps us to stand up, remove ourselves from the rubble, and build our lives again.

There are two ways we can receive this gift of opportunity. Some opportunities are recognized, found, and realized, while others are created. Both types are gifts and resources that can benefit you and others around you. This is why the gift of discernment is so important! You cannot heighten this gift without fine tuning your spiritual strength. When you learn to discern you will recognize, find, and realize when an opportunity presents itself.

Some opportunities are so common in certain places that it is easy to take them for granted. The opportunity for education in the United States is often overlooked and seen as a chore. Those in my home country are not always so blessed. Education is harder to come by. It is seen for the precious, valuable, and useful resource it is.

The opportunity for education is similar to networking. The opportunity for connections and relationships with people, and many more are often overlooked or taken for granted. When we use those that we are given, we can then create more choices that advance our lives.

My father took the opportunity for education and did his best, and he then provided me with the same chance to also receive an education. Not just me, but also his family, my siblings, and so on for generations. Always be aware of how good works help far more than we can fully understand and appreciate when engaged in those efforts.

In order to create more of these blessings and opportunities for ourselves and others, we need to do more than simply see those around us. We need to take positive action and active steps towards achieving those various goals.

But even before you can begin to take those steps, you need to have a belief in YOU.

We need to know that we can become something and that we can make things happen in our lives. This belief needs to happen before we can take steps that will create future opportunities. Action always follows belief. We create opportunities through action. Step by step, believe in yourself, think ahead, and follow through.

Even when there is something exciting right in front of us, so many shy away from greatness. Friendships, better jobs, higher pay, freedom, greater health, or the chance to serve another can all lead to a higher state of living. We think that for some reason, we aren't social enough, qualified enough, bold enough, or charitable enough. We imagine someone else could do it better, or that we can't make a real difference.

These thoughts are the ones that keep us trapped inside the rubble. It would have been so easy for me to give up as I waited to be rescued. But I couldn't do that. I heard the voices of the children fade away, so many disappeared from this life so quickly. But there was one voice asking me if we would live.

TiBlanc's voice. For him, there wasn't anyone else to tell him that he would live. That he will be ok. I didn't need to be smarter, more talented, or anything other than alive.

This child believed in me, even when I wanted to give up. And I made a promise that I had to keep. I believed that I could keep this promise. I believed that I was capable and it led me to more and greater opportunities that were created. When we believe that we can rise from the rubble, when we believe that we can earn the money to pay that bill, when we believe that we can learn how to do something new and challenging, we do those things. Fulfilling those goals will lead us to more opportunities that we create through our beliefs and actions. This is all proof that what we think about ourselves is powerful. If we all can see it in our mind and have the courage to say it to ourselves everyday, then we will manifest it.

Prepared to be led

It is hard to believe in things that we have not seen. We need to first see others accomplish things to know what is possible. This is why examples are so important. I would not be where I am today without many mentors and examples in my life. Looking to my father I saw that an education is possible for a poor boy from Haiti. I've been privileged enough to surround myself with amazing friends who have played a sacred role in my life and who taught me so much about building relationships with friends. We all need mentors to help shape our life for the better.

Having an example and a mentor can make all the difference between moderate success, and outstanding success. They foster a belief in ourselves when we might not be able to do so alone. Together, much more is possible. They show us how it is possible to rise from the rubble in our lives. They have done it themselves and they know the steps. This is why mentoring is a large part of my nonprofit organization **ARISE Project for Humanity.** If we want to change from being where we are to where we need to be, we need to have someone show us the way and it starts with mentoring.

As we learn these new steps to take, we increase our ability to believe in ourselves and find answers to problems. We start to create opportunities through our actions and relationships with others. No matter how big our mission in life may be, we have to first pre-pare ourselves with self confidence and learn the steps we must take.

My mission is to help rebuild Haiti, to help this generation discover the opportunities to create a robust and healthy Haiti and in the process prepare Haiti for the return of God. I truly believe that my life has been saved because God wanted me to be a part of Haiti's preparation for the second coming, for the new millenium.

We all have our own preparation to do. All of us have been prepared to help in different ways. By preparing yourself, you're going to be better able to prepare your country, your family, your community, and the people around you.

Testing Grounds

Having the opportunity to serve or being part of the Lord's work doesn't mean that things are going to be easy. It means that while you're working to accomplish great things, God will stand with you in every path along the way even if it seems hard, tough or impossible.

I believe that good things will happen in the midst of darkness and it's part of the plan.

No matter what tasks I have on my plate, I'm more dedicated to serving the people on the island because that's a big part of my mission on earth. I will do all I can to contribute to the change.

There is always going to be opposition when we are doing the Lord's work. There will always be challenges, but there will also be more than enough rewards. The gratitude we have for being a part of the bigger picture, the joy in the success of others, and seeing the goodness will always be greater and will always outlast the struggles we have. There will always be trials, but every struggle gives us purpose.

Each struggle we face makes us stronger and prepares our path to do the things we have been asked to do and the mission we have to fulfill. If we choose to start along this path, we can follow it through to the end when we remember the bigger picture. We become stronger every step of the way, making us more capable to accomplish the task, no matter how large or small.

Sometimes we may be successful, other times we may fail. But our attitude gives us a means of channeling this to future commitment and finding better ways to do things.

Just like the American inventor Thomas Edison once said about inventing the lightbulb, "I have not failed. I have found ten thousand ways that don't work." Edison could have given up, because it was too difficult or seemed impossible, but when we have a mission from God, we know it is possible.

We just have to figure out how to do it. I've learned along the way that the small voice inside my head, the nudge that pushes me to do something when I don't know why, that inner knowing that just comes without even being called (also known as my intuition) is a gift. A gift handed down to me through my ancestors.

It gives me the strength and wisdom I need to "figure it out." That saying, "go with your gut" isn't just a figure of speech. It's a truth that can't be unmatched, because if you listen to it, it will show you the way. That's why the power of believing in yourself is essential. You CAN, you WILL and you're READY.

THREE

RISING FROM THE RUBBLE

The story that changed my entire perspective and took me on a journey, at such a young age (16 years old). A journey that would lead me into finding my purpose, and help me understand why I survived that experience. To all the eleven orphans from the orphanage who laid helpless and hopeless next to me and died during the tragedy, I want you to know that although I couldn't hold out my arms or rescue you, my life's mission today is to ensure that my organization ARISE Project For Humanity will do all we can to keep every child in Haiti safe from all the mental constraints that create blockages.

"WILLIAMSON, your mom is outside waiting for you!"

Class had finished, and I was chatting with my friends and getting ready for our group study. I looked at the clock in surprise. My mother never came to get me this early. Every day, no exceptions, all of the students stayed to do homework together. Most days we were there until just before 6:00 PM. Since it was a private school, they expected so much from the students and that's why we had to get our homework done before leaving for the day. It was only 3:00 PM.

My school didn't look like the typical design of an American school. It was a four story apartment building and was a private school for the middle class citizens. Because it was a private school, all parents had to pick up the students in their private vehicles.

It was January and while it's considered the winter season, it is usually still very hot in the afternoon. Our school had a couple of basketball courts and a large soccer field. The entire school had 36 classes and around 30 students per class. The surrounding area of the school was all paved cement.

"What are you doing?" Kinson asked as I started to pack my things. He was one of my best friends at the Sapiens school. We'd been buddies since Kindergarten.

"My mom's outside waiting for me," I told him.

"Why? Doesn't she know you have home-work?"

I shrugged. If she was here to get me, she must have a reason. I waved good-bye to my classmates, never suspecting it would be the last time I would see each of their faces. I jogged down the stairs and out the front gate, for the last time.

"Hi, Mom." I said, as I opened the door of the red Isuzu Trooper and jumped into the seat next to hers. She smiled at me and began down the road. "I'm going to take you to the orphanage to work with the children for a while, all right? You can do your homework there." I nodded and looked out the window at my classmates. That was the last time I ever saw them.

Though she didn't tell me at the time, my mom had been at work, like always, and repeatedly had a feeling that she needed to come pick me up. So, she did. That's how Haitian mothers are. They have these feelings about their children, and they act on those instincts, even if they don't make sense in their brains. And we, as their children, don't question it. That's why I didn't ask my mother about the change in plans. She must have had that feeling.

I loved going to my parents' orphanage. The children were always so excited to see me. They loved telling me about their school work, their food, who hadn't showered on any given day, and who had been naughty. There was one boy in particular who was my little shadow. His name was TiBlanc. He was eleven and he followed me everywhere I went.

When I walked into the orphanage TiBlanc was right there waiting for me. "Williamson! Hey, Will! You're here early!"

"Yeah, man. I wanted to spend some time with you guys." I slapped him on the back, and walked into the room where the other twelve children were playing.

"Williamson!" They all ran to me, some clinging to my legs, others pulling on my shirt, trying to show me pages of artwork, or tell me stories about who had shirked their schoolwork, or who had only gotten a 4 on their exams. (*The haitian grading scale is as such; 9/10 highest, 8-7/10 good, 5.5-6.5/10 average, 3-5/10 low.*)

I smiled as TiBlanc continued on with his update and adoringly looked up at me. It felt good to be someone's hero. To be a positive role model and "big brother" to these kids who didn't see their families much, meant everything to me. I loved it. I loved them and didn't mind setting my homework aside.

We talked and played until I remembered that I needed to fill the water tanks. In Haiti, there are large tanks on top of each house. They hold the water we use for cooking, cleaning, bathing, and flushing the toilet. With TiBlanc following me, we gathered buckets and went to the spigot in the front yard, filled the buckets and took them up onto the roof to dump into the tanks.

When we were finished, we put the buckets away and were about to walk back into the schoolroom, when the ground swayed and began to slip from under our feet. TiBlanc looked at me, fear and confusion in his eyes.

"What's happening?" he yelled.

It took me a few seconds to realize what was going on, but when I did, I pulled him in front of my chest and lowered him to the ground, dropping to my elbows and knees.

As we dropped the building completely collapsed around us. Pain. I had never felt so much pain ever in my life.

I was on my stomach, face pressed into the dirt, rubble weighing me down. My right wrist was throbbing, layers of cement pinned my left arm and shoulder to the ground, and I could feel blood, sticky and warm, as it trickled down my face.

TiBlanc was under me, crying and yelling. He was alive. My body had taken the brunt of the trauma, but he was hurt, too, folded at a painfully unnatural angle. "Williamson," he said, his voice trembling and terrified, "are we going to make it out alive?"

"Yes, we're going to make it," I said firmly.

"Are we going to die?"

"We're not going to die."

In the following twenty-eight hours, I would tell him that, over and over. At times,

I was far from believing it myself. I was broken, I could literally feel my body coming apart in different places, though I had stopped feeling it in others. I could see my own left hand, but I thought it was someone else's because I had no sensation. I could feel sharp shards of stone embedded and pressing into my head. How would anyone be able to get me out, let alone put me back together again?

I could hear the other twelve children crying and yelling. I knew they were hurt and afraid and I wished I could comfort them. But I couldn't move. After a while, I started to hear voices. They were faint, but I could hear my father. He was looking for me.

"Williamson!" TiBlanc said, "They're here. Call them! Call them! Tell them we're here!"

"Dad, we're here! I'm here! We're alive!" I yelled and screamed until my throat was hoarse. But my voice refused to carry through the layers of cement and stone and metal. He couldn't hear me. He couldn't physically hear my voice by the flesh of his ears, but later I found out that his spiritual ears were ringing very loudly. He knew I was ok. His inner knowing said that I was there, alive, and waiting for him and the others to pull me out.

From LDS Church blog
churchofjesuschrist.org/inspiration/finding-god-while-buried-in-rubble?lang=eng

This picture above describes the lights that come from the dark. The hours of friends and neighbors trying to dig to get me out, the hope that comes when I see the outside begin to show. But what most people didn't know is that my left hand was trapped too. Since the earthquake, my wrist has been broken and so many other injuries in that arm but I still do all I can to rely on the right arm. Our darkest time can turn around and be our shiniest or brightest time.

My dad was there the whole night. I could hear him working, I could hear him asking others to help him. When he was silent, I could imagine him sleeping on the rubble of the building, just for a few moments, so he would have the strength to keep going. That night, one by one, the other children grew silent. I knew what the silence meant. And as they grew silent, the air, struggling to permeate through the rubble, grew cold. Haiti doesn't get cold.

In those moments, in that gap of silence and rigid coldness, I remember talking to each of them. A meeting of sorts was held right there under the rubble. Right in their moments of crossing to the otherside, they and I had a meeting. Maybe it was about my destiny. I don't know if it was a dream, or real, but I spoke to each one of them, one by one. While we were all under that building I had a very special conversation with the children who didn't make it out. While I can't remember specifics of the lengthy discussion or the words that were spoken, I can remember the symphony of voices, I can remember them saying goodbye towards the end, and then I recall actually waking up or coming to consciousness. It was like I was coming out of a deep slumber. Right then I decided that I needed to pray.

Even though I was Catholic at the time, I wasn't very religious and didn't know much about God. Praying wasn't something I had ever done before.

"Jesus," I said, out loud, "please let me live. Please. Please! Let me live!" I prayed and I begged harder than I ever have before and soon found myself making a deal with God. "If you let me live, I will serve you for the rest of my life. Please let me live!"

The destruction to the buildings that were affected by the earthquake was truly due to the lack of proper building regulations. Had the building standards been more defined and updated, they may have been able to withstand the brunt of the disaster. Some of Haiti's most prominent landmarks in the city of Port-au-Prince were just about damaged beyond repair. Those areas included; The Cathedral, National Palace, United Nations Headquarters, National Penitentiary, and the Parliament building. Back in 2008, Port-au-Prince, suffered two huge tropical storms that had already weakened the city's building frameworks. Though a couple of years later, the city was still recovering and not prepared for the earthquake's damage. The efforts of

Haitian citizens and international aid organizations to provide medical assistance, food, and water to survivors was hindered due to the failing electrical power system, loss of communication lines, and road blocked with debris.

A week after the event, still little had been done to reach Port-au-Prince, after another week, supplies were finally dispensed among the suffering people, but the supplies and aid was scattered. The teams of rescuers, which had already freed over 100 people, ceased their efforts about two weeks after the disaster. Remarkably, there were still occasional recoveries of people who had managed to hang in there and slowly found their way out. It was estimated that nearly one-third of the country's total population was eternally affected by the 2010 heart-wrenching earthquake.

Over one million Haitian citizens were left homeless. The remains and upkeep of the land was so displaced, people were forced to make do in donated tents and were given materials that were found thrown about. The lack of food and supplies took such a devastating toll on the economy. People fought each other, stole, pillaged, and did all they could desperately think of to gather supplies for their suffering families. The despoil became more prominent as there were thousands of prisoners that escaped from the penitentiary. Also in the second week of the turbulence, the Haitian government did structure relocation programs to assist with reducing crowded areas infested with unsanitary conditions.

Hospitals were useless, survivors were forced to wait days, even weeks for treatment. Morgues quickly reached their capacity levels which resulted in dead bodies being thrown in designated areas around the wrecked streets. Saved to be burned later. The bodies had to be burned to mask the smell of decaying flesh. The impulsive filtering and humane disposal of the bodies in such frenzies made it impossible for casualty counts to be made. Haitain officials did estimate a number of about 222,570, even though there was absolutely no way to verify that number was accurate. It has still been estimated that hundreds of thousands more perished under the earthquake attack.

Weeks after the damages, more deaths arose due to the serious injuries that went untreated in the absence of medical treatment and supplies. Children were left without parents, abandoned in the streets, and made vulnerable to abuse and trafficking. Although adoptions of Haitian children by foreign nationals, particularly in the United States, was facilitated, the process was slow. As the Haitian authorities wanted to make absolute sure the children did not have living relatives.

My own family, as well, was devastated by the earthquake in 2010. My family home and all we knew was destroyed. We had to also live with the savage details of the way the bodies that laid slain from the earthquake had been mercilessly handled. Bodies were thrown away like trash. There was no proper way to dispose of them. No burials, no homage or respect— nothing. Some were shoved into collapsed and abandoned buildings, then set on fire, burned. Burning the bodies was the only way officials saw fit to control the decaying and smell. So much trauma and loss the people had to continue experiencing during the aftermath. Even after losing loved ones, friends, and peers, we were forced to witness the barbaric removal of their bodies from the rubble.

I felt that life as we knew it was over. There was no water, no food, no work. The officials that worked the streets to keep order, quarried us all to stand in lines to receive 1 bag of cracks. Cracks were like small dry cookies that were filled with nutrients to keep you alive. You had 1 bag for each member of your family. In order to get the bags you have to stand in line for 6 hours. If you wanted more, you would have to go back to the line and stand another 6 hours. It was torture to say the least, BUT there was still hope. That was the beginning of a new chapter in my life.

A LETTER TO TIBLANC

*The little boy who was
pinned underneath me the entire time*

Hello TiBlanc,

Mesperew anfòm? mwen panse avèw chak jou nan lavim. Mwen paka imajine kòmanw te santiw pandanw te anba gwosè kay sa ki tap pezew pandan tout tan sa. Tout pwa m ak fòs mwen te sou ou ew pat menm ka respire.... Mwen konnen sa te difisil anpil pou ou menm konnen tou ke mwen ak ou pat pou kont nou. Se si pat pou ou, ki tap relem nan nonm viretounen pandan nou 2 a anba gwo kay la, si se pat pou ou, mwen pa tap la jodia. Paskem sonje kòman mwen te fatige, swaf, grangou ak egzòste. Mwen imajine si m ta manke abandone, tout bagay fini, lavi nou, espwa moun ki ap ede nou soti yo ak anpil lòt ankò...

Mwen sou tèt ou, si mwen te abandone, tout bagay fini e TiBlanc ta fè menm bagay la paske mwen se te sèl moun ak sèl fason pou fè li sove e mwen te santi ke pifò moun deyò a te plis konsène sou lavi mwen pase lavi pa TiBlanc antanke yon timoun òfelina.

Mwen pa t 'kapab abandone! non mwen pa t

'kapab! ou te rezon pou m te siviv eksperyans sa e bay tout mwen menm pou nou rete anvi, mwen konnen si m te kontinye, se pa sèlman lavi m, se yon lòt lavi ki te anba m, lavi w Tiblan te tèlman presye pou mwen pou m te wè m abandone chans sa ke mwen te genyen. pou sove nou de. Mwen sonje te gen yon moman kote m mande w pou pou w sispann pale paske l t ap fatige w anpil e l te ka pran souf ou rapid siw fatige, men ou pa janm sispann e kounye a mwen konnen poukisa ou pa janm sispann. Paske lide w pou w viv te diferan de mwen. Mwen te kapab tande vwa yo sou lòt bò a kap di m 'pou sispann itilize enèji ak vwa mwen e se te yon vwa espirityèl ki te tankou yon vwa yon granmoun fanm ki di m' kenbe kalm mwen epi trankil pou konsève kèk enèji.

Mesperew sonje chak segond nou pase ansanm anba gwo kay la, yo pat fasil pou simonte men nou te simonte yo e mwen kwè ke si nou kapab simonte moman sa, nou kapab simonte nenpòt lòt moman nan lavi nou. Nenpòt kotew ye nan laviw, mwen vlew konnen ke w espesyal e kew gen gwo misyon sou tèt ou ak gwo potorik gwoup byen detèmine pou edew reyalize ak akonpli misyon sa yo.

Frèw, Wil

A LETTER TO TIBLANC

The little boy who was
pinned underneath me the entire time

ENGLISH VERSION

Hello TiBlanc,

I hope you are doing well. I think about you every day of my life. I can't imagine how you felt when you were under the rubble. All my weight and strength were on you and I couldn't even breathe. I know it was very difficult for you to know that you and I were not alone. If it weren't for you, who would have talked to me while we were under the building? If it wasn't for you, I wouldn't be here today. I remember how tired, thirsty, hungry, and exhausted I was. I wonder if I would have given up if you weren't there.

In my head, if I gave up, everything would end and TiBlanc would not survive because I was the only person and the only way to make it out safe. I felt that mostly because most people out there were more concerned about my life than the life of TiBlanc as an orphan child.

I knew I couldn't give up, I just couldn't! You deserved to survive this experience and I needed to give all of me for us to stay alive. I know if I continued, not just my life would be spared, but also yours too. Your life, TiBlanc, was so precious to me and I didn't want to give up that chance to save it.

I'm sure you remember every second we spent together under the building. They were not easy to overcome but we overcame them and I believe that if we can overcome that moment, we can overcome any other moment in our lives. Wherever you are in life, I want you to know that you are special and that you have a great mission and a group of people from the other side who will help you accomplish that mission.

Your brother, Wil

FOUR

MY CONVERSION

My spiritual journey has been a big part of what's led me to where I am in life. My earthquake story has led me to seek for more spiritual growth and to have a better relationship with God to know how I can keep the promise that I made with him.

REMEMBER THE PROMISE I made with God while I was under that building. "If you save me, I will serve you." Those words played through my head constantly in the days and weeks after the earthquake. I reached out to God to know why he had saved my life, when so many others had died. After the earthquake our family lived in a tent because our house was destroyed. Many people lived in tents, not just those whose houses were destroyed but also those who didn't dare be under a roof that could possibly collapse on them. The anxiety and fear that it had sprung in us was real. Most people wanted to sleep in the street or in a tent in case any other rumblings happened and the buildings shook again. I look back on that time and remember the heaviness all around me but there was also a fire deep inside me to learn more.

Three months after the earthquake, I met a friend who would come by my tent to hang out. We were in a big camp of tents and his family was also in the same camp. Eventually

I learned that he went to church and he started inviting me to come to activities with him. I loved the feelings I felt there. I was introduced to two missionaries. When they invited me to read The Book of Mormon, I was so thirsty to know for myself that I read it in just fifteen days. I had some sacred spiritual experiences while reading and praying in that small tent.

I knew that God was guiding me to where I needed to be to serve him. I was baptized into The Church of Jesus Christ of Latter-day Saints in July, on my birthday, six months after the earthquake.

I was raised in a Christian home. Growing up, I was taught the principles from the Bible and how to be a good person. But there is a difference between knowledge and belief. Before the earthquake, I knew about God and His son, Jesus Christ. After the earthquake, I actually connected with God and His son Jesus Christ. I truly got to know them. Everything I had known about God and my spirituality I realized I had taken for granted. Knowledge is having information about a particular topic. Belief is more than knowing the information, it involves the heart. It means there is faith and trust in the information.

The earthquake had changed my whole perspective on life. Why was I the only one from my school who was spared? Why was I one of the only two to survive from the orphanage? Why did God spare my life? What was my calling in life that I needed to fulfill? How was I going to keep the promise I made to God when I told him I would serve him if He saved my life?

The earthquake helped me to experience this shift. I experienced a change of heart that led to a deep and lasting conversion. After the earthquake, I was guided to where the Lord needed me to be in order to serve him in a greater capacity. God was with me, even at the worst and hardest points of being buried under the rubble. He heard my promise to him. My heart was touched and changed. I started to feel more connected to God as a result of this conversion and that connection allowed me to be guided to where I need to be in order to become who I need to be.

The seed God is trying to plant in us often comes from someone else, someone near us. As long as we try our hardest to listen and connect, to get to know those around us, the Lord will be able to use them, whether they are aware of it or not. He wants to plant that seed, that faith, that hope, that miraculous thing within us. This seed can only come from God. And if we pay attention, we'll be able to see that he is doing that right now.

I'm grateful for spiritual influences in my life and in my communities. These people have influenced my life in such a way that I know that the gifts and talents I have came from God. They're things that he planted within me. So, I'm using today to bless my nation, to bless those around me, to bless my family.

I knew that I was the seed planted. I knew that I was the seed that God planted up under the rubble. Over time, my conversion has become more and more deep. That conversion is my connection to God. I work to serve him every day. The earthquake was the first step in me recognizing God's hand in my life, but it has been a steady and continual growth since then. As I continue to serve him, I continue to see miracles happen in my life.

Over time, I have come to see the earthquake as something so much more than just a tragedy. While it certainly had devastating effects for many in my home country and in my life, it has also served a greater purpose.

If I could go back in time and the earthquake never happened, I would not be the same person I am today. I have become so much more, and so much better because of the life that I have lived. If it weren't for the hard things, I would have had no driving force in my life that would push me to be changed and transformed.

When we open our eyes to see the good in what has happened, we can continue to grow. Yes, I had something terrible happen to me. So many have stories like that. Hard things happen. But as a result of these hard things, there were opportunities for good things to happen. It is when everything falls apart that we can start to build something better.

I don't know what my life would be like if I hadn't made this promise to God to serve him. I do know that my life would be different. The life I am living now is so much better than I could have dreamed. I would not have the quality of life I do, if I had not turned my life over to God. In turn, I would not have given my life to God if I had not been trapped underneath that building for twenty-eight hours. The hardest times often yield the biggest blessings.

It does take moving from victim to survivor to victor. In our lowest moments, we have to see the good in order to turn them into a tool that will help us rise from the rubble. The earthquake was just the beginning. The earthquake was a simple seed that was planted all those years ago. The earthquake converted me into a new being and prepared me for a divine purpose.

FIVE

THE LADY IN THE BLUE DRESS

The lady who has been my guardian. Someone that I never knew while she was alive but I am grateful that she's been assigned to watch over me.

URING ONE OF THOSE moments of suffering under the earthquake, in an instant, I saw a lady in a blue dress. She was standing far away in the corner. My eyes felt heavy, there was vomit all over my face, and I think I had passed out. I could hear TiBlanc continuing to say, over and over "Are we going to make it? Are we going to make it?" Before I could answer him again, the lady in the blue dress said to me, "Hush. Be quiet. Save your energy. You're going to make it out."

I felt the cinder blocks on my back lighten and instead of the cold press of cement, I felt a warm body on my back, comforting me. I felt strengthened. I didn't know it then, but what I would later find out is that my grandmother, who I had never known, (my mother didn't even remember her because she died when my mother was only three years old), was there to help TiBlanc and I that day.

Even now to this very day, during the times when I need emotional, physical, or mental support, that is when I feel my grandmother the most. Just as she was there that horrific day under the rubble, today she remains my rock when I feel pressured by mental constraints. She spiritually offers the support that helps me process any grief, anguish, sadness, or whatever tries to discourage my peace mentally.

My grandmother's presence always feels like a warm blanket over me. I can feel her hug, her arms, her chin as it nuzzles into the crook of my neck, right on the left side of my chin. It's like she's hugging me from behind and has settled her face next to my left side so she can see what I'm writing. She approves of this work.

When my mom found out that I was underneath the building, she snapped. She was sure that I was dead and she didn't want to be there when they found me. She couldn't bear it. She was the one who got me out of school early and dropped me off at the orphanage. Was all of this her fault? She was walking aimlessly, crying, and screaming for her dead child. She walked far from the orphanage, to a park on the other side of town, and sat down on a bench to sob and mourn.

Soon, that same lady in the blue dress with a smile and kind eyes approached (*the same lady whose voice I heard, telling me to preserve my energy while laying on top of TiBlanc.*) Anyone watching might have mistaken them for sisters. She sat next to my mother and said, "Don't worry. They're going to get him out. Be patient." Right at that moment, my mom had her confirmation that I was going to make it.

We all have a "lady in a blue dress" in our lives. Maybe not specifically a lady, could be a man in the flannel shirt, or a dog with a green collar. The point I'm trying to make is that our spirit team is alive, well, and ready to stand up for you. So you can preserve your energy, be calm in the storm, and not be afraid in the fire, because your team will always ensure that justice prevails for you.

Sometimes we may not see or hear them, but I truly believe that those who are called to minister to us in spirit are all around us and they are always on time when we are in danger, when we are in mourning, in sadness, in anger, when we need endurance, and even when we are happy. They are there to let us know how very proud they are. As we go through life's many tests and climb past those tests, we are rewarded by our ancestors with a higher ranking in the spirit. Our spiritual gifts are heightened to lengths we never imagined possible.

One of my greatest strengths has always been endurance. My paternal grandfather was the same. He was a hard worker and always known for his ability to press forward, no matter how strenuous or hard the work was. When I work out, or go for a run in the mornings, I can always hear his footsteps behind me, willing me forward. "Go faster, Williamson. Take deep breaths, you can do it, you are strong, you are powerful."

I can keep going and going without getting tired. I can feel him there, sometimes it's like he's carrying me. Believe, brothers and sisters, that your lady, man, or pet... is there in spirit, cheering you on every step of the way. They could be blocking the path from your enemies to enter or raging war in the spirit to keep your mind clear of spiritual warfare. Call on them when you feel weary, as you say your prayers to God, they will be there with you, knees and heads bowed right along with you.

I can think of so many times, my grandmother and her favorite blue dress have come to help me. Little miracles happen all the time to me. Once while out of town, I was rushing, and locked my keys in the car. It was going to cost so much money to get a locksmith to unlock the door, so much time, we needed to get going. I kept thinking, "What am I going to do? What should I do?" The car door had a keyless entry pad. You could punch in a code. This was a rental car, so I couldn't remember the code. I decided right then, to bow my head and say a prayer. I asked God to help me get into the car. I opened my eyes and just pressed the first set of numbers that came to mind. The door opened.

My wife is never surprised when miracles like this happen to me. She has been around me long enough to know "my faith can move mountains", as she says. So many times we take the small victories in our lives as coincidences. We blow them off like they're an everyday thing—like we're entitled to luck. There are no lucky stars, or superstitions, but only supernatural events that are occurring, because the spirit is present. These things are happening because your spirit team is answering the call. The calls, and instructions from God to aid in your prayers being answered.

SIX

THE PROMISE KEEPER

This book is a promise I made 3 years ago to bring my story to life, I truly believe that we all have a story and only you own your story, no one else. You are unique and no one can replicate you. Never be discouraged, never allow others opinions to control what you think or what you do. Never accept defeat. Never let go. These common factors will keep you together with the promises you set to fulfill.

MADE A PROMISE TO GOD while I was under the rubble of the earthquake that if He saved me, I was going to serve him. I didn't know exactly what that meant at the moment, only that I needed to pray. That prayer provided the relief and the strength I would need to endure until the rescuers reached me.

Each breath I took was a reminder to me that God was keeping his promise. I was still alive. Not only was I alive, but I was able to rise from the rubble of the building, and in life. I made a promise to God, but God kept his promise to me first. He allowed me to live, so I knew I also had to keep my promise.

As I studied more about God, I learned that this is called a covenant. When we make a promise to God and God makes a promise to us, a two-way promise, or covenant is formed. If I wanted to receive the blessing of life, I had also to fulfill my promise. If my promise is not kept, God doesn't have to keep his promise either. My very life depended on my ability to follow through when I committed to this promise. God saw my heart, and knew that I would do my best.

These experiences have taught me so much about the importance of keeping my promises and commitments. God does not expect me to be perfect, only that I try my best. I truly believe that if we do what we can, God will do what we can't. So often we underestimate what our best is. We are capable of doing so much more than we know if we are willing to give one hundred percent in all that we do. Not just the things that we like to do, or what we think is important, but in everything.

As human beings, we are not perfect. There are times when we may fall and fail. But each of these experiences teach us a little bit more about ourselves, our talents and capabilities. We each have our own unique gifts and talents that we use as we go through this life. Each promise we make, whether to God, to others, or even to ourselves, can help us discover what those are. These promises also give us the opportunity to learn and develop new skills and talents that we can then use.

We don't always know ourselves enough to know what we are capable of, what we love and enjoy, or what we want out of life. I found myself rising from a spiritual rubble when I was able to start making, and more importantly keeping, promises to myself. I discovered more about myself as I made promises to myself and to God.

Take Action

In order to keep the promise I had made, I had to take action and follow through. If I was going to serve God, I first had to figure out what that meant. What does it mean to serve God, and what does He want me to do? These were the first steps that I had to figure out if I wanted to keep my promise.

This is also very important for any promise we make, not just the promises we make to God. When we make a promise, we have made a commitment to follow through. Life can be really hard, but when we do not keep our promises, it becomes much harder. The inability to commit holds us back from so many of life's greatest blessings.

Promises are hard to make. It is so difficult to follow through to the end, but that doesn't mean we shouldn't make promises at all. We can only do the best we can, and we don't always know what that is. This means that making promises does come with a certain amount of risk. There are results and consequences for every action we take and promises are no exception.

The best part about keeping my promise to God is how He usually over-delivers. Yes, He spared my life that day in Haiti, but I have been blessed with so much more afterwards as I have continued to serve him. He has continued to bless me with greater blessings than I could have dreamed, such as my beautiful wife and children, connections with wonderful people, and the ability to continue to grow and improve.

When we commit to actions, especially actions that were the fulfilling of a promise, we receive so much more than we give. This is not only true with God, but also again, with ourselves and others. It is the principle of synergy. In essence, because synergy requires a joint collaboration of components we must first build the system that is going to catapult us into action. With promises to God comes determination, structure, and discipline. You must strip away all the parts of you that want to fall into the trap of self doubt and low self worth.

The same boundaries we create with negative outside influences are the same boundaries we create with ourselves. Belief and the will to choose the right are absolutely necessary to make it up the mountain. It is important to know that nothing is happening to you. Everything is happening for you. Every no, every up, every down, it has all contributed to who you are. It's up to you how you choose to use your experiences. How hard you choose to work and the sacrifices you choose to make are all a part of your test of fate. The power of your convictions is a must. If you don't believe it, then who will? You have to stand up, stand your ground, make hard decisions, wipe tears away, and if you have to lose any blood on the way to salvation then that is what you do.

Synergy

The Oxford dictionary defines synergy as, "the interaction or cooperation of two or more organizations, substances, or other agents to produce a combined effect greater than the sum of their separate effects," or one plus one is three. Maybe it equals greater, like five or ten. When we work together and promise to fulfill our commitments, we are able to make something that is greater than what we could do on our own.

Take for example, the writing of this book. I have the stories and the thoughts and principles in my head, but I have never written a book before. It was very important to me and my mission. And with my busy schedule it got very difficult for me to make real progress on getting it written. So I reached out to a friend who is a writer.

This has been a great experience for both of us. When she promised to help me, I received what I needed to complete my book. This helps me to fulfill my promises that I made and allows me to move forward with my mission. In return, this friend can better pursue her dreams and her mission. Without the commitment to follow through, this book would not have been written as quickly, and I am grateful for her. Through the commitments and promises, we are each able to achieve more.

On the opposite end, when we break promises, we are not able to realize what could have happened. We make promises every day, and must fulfill those promises. When I moved to the US in 2015, I made a promise to stay focused and do all I can to take every opportunity that came my way. I was determined to keep that promise and still today I keep my focus so high and I can't remember the last time I took a nap. Not because it isn't necessary for my health but because I had things to do, missions to discover, work to get done, dreams to chase, life to empower, places to go, daylight to see, so I can't pause now.

They have more hope for something better in their lives. Keeping promises may start with me, but the results of keeping that promise are endless and continue on forever. They will last long after our life is over.

One thing that is often overlooked when it comes to promises is the promises we make to ourselves. We make promises that are broken far more often. A good friend of mine once told me her story about becoming a morning person. She used to hate getting up in the mornings and had to set several alarms to get her out of bed. One of her mentors once said something that shook her to the core. "I believe that it's not confidence that leads to success, it's successful behavior that leads to confidence." She realized she had been breaking a promise to herself to wake up. It was the successful behavior that led her to trust herself, and that led to even greater things.

I have also seen the benefits of waking up early. With the promises I have made to God and to myself, I have a lot of work to do. My sweet wife is often telling me when I am tired that I should take a nap. However, coming to the U.S. and having to learn English and so many other things, I often feel behind. I do not want to feel behind, knowing that someone else is getting what I am working for. .

If we don't make promises to ourselves, there will be no change in our life. It may be a small thing like waking up when you say you will wake up. It may be a big promise like dedicating your life to God. Everyone has a different path, but each path will always include promises. Those promises will change your life. What is a promise you have to make that will change your life forever?

Beliefs

One of the biggest factors in our ability to keep our promises is our beliefs. I am not shy about my belief in God; I believe that depending on a higher power does so much for us in helping us to keep our promises. As was mentioned before, part of this is due to knowing that God will keep his promises to me when I keep my promises to him.

However, there is also a deeper level that we can look into with this. There are two ways that a belief in a higher power (I call him God, but feel free to use your own choice of words) will help us in this act of keeping promises. Not just to him, but to others around us as well.

The first way is knowing that something will happen when we keep our promises. No one wants to put in a lot of hard work and see nothing come as a result. We want to know that our efforts are not in vain. Knowing that there is a divine power that stands with us helps us to know that all of our best efforts will be rewarded. God is a perfect being and as such will always fulfill His promises. This is why I make promises to God. Things may not always turn out according to my plan, but I know it will always be the best possible path for me.

When we put the sacred and divine first, all things work out for our good. Even when people do not fulfill their promises to me, God makes a way for the thing to happen, because He knows I am doing my part. He knows that I serve Him and seek to help and serve His children.

The second way is having a connection to greater wisdom and insight that comes from within us. It is hard for us to decipher what thoughts and feelings are from God or from our own heads. But I trust in myself and know that if the thought is good, it is worth pursuing.

Human nature makes us seek safety and comfort. But this does not show us our true nature and what we are capable of. At Harvard in the 1950's, Dr. Curt Richter performed a study to see how long rats could swim in a pool of water. It was not the most humane study, but it did show some amazing results.

On average, the rats would stop swimming after just fifteen minutes after being placed in the water and start to drown. Dr. Richter would then pull them out of the water before they did and give them a few minutes of rest. Then the rats were placed right back in the water. Only this time, the rats continued to swim for sixty hours. Not minutes. HOURS.

The conclusion was that the rats simply believed they would be rescued again, and pushed themselves to hang on just a little bit longer. Far beyond what was previously thought possible. The difference was astounding.

How often have you wanted to give up and

pushed yourself just a little bit farther and stretched your mind just a little bit more? In life, we are continuously learning, absorbing information all around us. It may be information on how to grow healthy crops, it may be how to read, it may be how to treat others around us. But sometimes, we don't always learn the correct information. We think we know what we are capable of self mastery, but God knows better than we do what lies within us.

Because God knows us so well as His children, he will help push us to become better, even when it is uncomfortable and we don't think we can do it. Trusting our own feelings makes us fall short. We give up too soon.

We are pushed and stretched in order to grow. Eventually, the growth and discomfort become more comfortable. I'm used to trying new things now, because I know the formula that will bring me success. I know that when I want to do something, I find a mentor to teach me and guide me. I promise to do what is asked of me, and I know that I will have success. Not always right away. It takes time to learn and grow, and I make mistakes at first. But then I became better. I can swim longer than I thought.

When we keep our promises, good things always happen. When we put forth effort, others will see it. Not just the person that we promised. I have had many opportunities come because people know that I will keep my promises. Keeping our promises helps us to rise up above where we are currently. It leads to opportunities, to connections and relationships, and it leads us to a greater sense of purpose. If I hadn't kept that first promise to God to serve him, I would never have risen from the rubble of that orphanage. I have seen how far my promises have taken me, and I know that this is a principle that will work. It is very dear to my heart.

SEVEN

THE POWER OF CHOICES

The choices we make in our daily life will determine our future. A deep inner knowing and hemisphere of confidence has to be embraced while taking on life's decisions. We have to focus on spiritual growth, and in that process we'll realize that the decisions we make will create a push and pull effect on all areas of our lives. We will outgrow people, places, and things so that we can better spread our wings and learn to fly independently. It's necessary that we remain humble to our abilities, never feel as though the world owes you something simply because you have a gift. Unlock your greatest potential by making the choice to take action. Live in the present moment always. Being brilliant or talented does not exonerate you from hard work. Use your power to make great choices, choices that will carry you through the test of time. Choices that will affect not only your life, but the lives of every thing and person that merely touches your presence.

THIS WAS A PIVOTAL MOMENT for me, because while I felt vulnerable to the building that was crushing me, I still had to make a choice. I had to choose to to either rely on God or torture myself with the doubt and fear that I wouldn't make it. Survival mode was ON. I was going to make it, because it was already written. Through all the pain, hearing my own bones crushing down, feeling that I wasn't going to be able to take one more ounce of pain, but still. I breathed on, hearing TiBlanc say, Are we going to make it, Will? I was still able to answer him. The choice wasn't mine, but the choice to have faith that my suffering wouldn't be in vain, was mine and mine alone. My faith was the greatest choice I'd ever make then, and will ever make now.

Growing up in Haiti, making the right choices was my biggest challenge. I had to make hard, but important decisions every-day. I had great mentors that helped me make great decisions that would shape my life for the better, and that helped create the bridge to my success. One of the key principles I learned growing up is to love and respect those around me. Love was the essence of my journey in Haiti, and continues to be, even now.

The choices you make right now will determine where your life is going to be in five to ten years. I truly believe that the choices I made five years ago are the ones that carried me to where I am today in my life. I've also learned that while being impulsive and impatient aren't always the best option, sometimes in life, we must take risks.

No one can receive a high return on their investment if they're not willing to take high level risks. That's why having a good balance between knowing when to pull back and knowing when to "move now" is one of the key elements to my success. We cannot always wait around until the perfect moment. There will never be a perfect moment when moving with Spirit.

Having faith and belief in oneself means not worrying about having enough money, not worrying about having enough food, not worrying about how you look, where you will sleep, where you will live, how you will live, most importantly not worrying about what everyone else thinks about the moves you make. Making a powerful choice means being strategic in the way we trust that as long as we're choosing to covenant with God, then he will provide all that is necessary, when the time is right. We need not worry about worldly pleasures. Our fate lies in the hands of walking by faith and not by sight. When God wants it, God provides.

The choices we make are also prompted by our perception. Knowing when to cease an opportunity that's presented. Keeping a clear, concise, focused mind at all times, never giving up, and standing your ground, when the adversary battles to discourage and stress you out, are all factors that make up the level of our success.

We must also remember that choosing is one thing, but choosing the right things is essential. As humans, we are gracefully given the power of free will. Discretion is of the utmost importance. Understanding our moral responsibility will unlock an array of blessings along our journey. In every choice we make, our moral and ethical judgment creates a force within humanity that we must learn to navigate.

When it comes to making things happen in my life, I have never needed to wait to be fully ready to make things happen, every time I feel the power of my choices, I go all in to make it happen. I truly believe that my choices are what will get me places and as long as I feel the power within my choices. Nothing will stop me from going after it.

My Mother's Choices

The living room was bare, much like the rest of my mom's house. The last of the furniture had been sold. The money— every nickel and dime that was either earned or borrowed— went from my mom's hand to mine that day. "Pursue your dreams," my mom said. "Above all, trust God."

Then I left her. I left other family members and friends, too. I did not know when I would ever see them again. I left Haiti, the only home I ever knew, for the United States. This was the hardest decision I ever had to make, but I was compelled by a greater vision.

I came to Utah where Blacks make up less than two percent of the state's population, according to the U.S. Census Bureau. Here, it was common for someone that I'd met for the first time to call me, "the Black Haitian kid." That didn't bother me in the sense that I was proud to be both. I'd think, "Thank you for seeing me. Yes, I'm black. And thank you for recognizing the beautiful country I'm from."

It was annoying, however, to be called "the black Haitian kid" by someone I already knew. After meeting a few times, it made sense to me that by now they should call me by my name. Names are important to people, and I do my best to remember them correctly. Like anyone else, I enjoy people knowing my name. Not only that, at twenty-one years old, I was a man, no longer a kid.

I felt like I was asked a million times in each conversation, "What are you saying?" People didn't understand me, either. I'd think, "I'll repeat myself. Like you said, I have a thick accent. I hope we can chat and connect."

Any hopes for connecting were generally shot down and people would sneer, laugh, or imitate my accent. I was hurt. Potential connections failed. I remained alone. I observed immediate mistrust from others. I would reach out to people, but their hesitation would cut me off mid sentence.

I extended my hand out—I saw my black skin, the ebony that swathed the very hands that built the Americas— again and again and again. Eventually, I was able to meet people who were not only willing, but happy to be my friend. I finally had more connections here and we were able to understand one another better.

When I came to Utah, it wasn't easy to get the basic things that I needed. I had to work hard for them, I had to try harder than others did just for the bare minimum. But I know that the choices I made—to work harder, to try harder, changed my life.

One of the other choices I made was choosing to further my education. At the time I made that choice, I didn't have anything. I came here with nothing. No English, no money to survive, no place to stay, but I knew that was the best chance I had. If I chose right, I could make something out of my life.

I lived at my bishop's house and chose to go to the library to study English every day. At that time, my English was very bad, so I had a choice to make. I could do everything in my power to learn the language and hope that doors would open because of that choice, or I could wait for something to happen to me.

Wait for someone to offer me money. Wait for someone to do the work for me. Be a victim of my circumstances. I chose to be proactive and work. I made the choice to further my education, to learn, to study, to accept criticism from other people about my English. And that choice helped me to improve my pronunciation, to expand my vocabulary, to correct the things I didn't say right, so I could speak better.

Because I worked to learn English, I was able to pass the TOEFL (English Language Proficiency Test), which led me to Brigham Young University–Idaho.

I was reminded by some wonderful friends that I needed to use my life story to help the Haitian people, my people. I wanted to make my first trip to Haiti, but I was scared because I didn't have enough money to spend on a trip at that time. Even so, I knew I must! You know that feeling when you know you are supposed to do something but this scary voice never leaves you alone? It is because they know what you can accomplish the moment you start creating what you were born to do.

The things we most want in life, the things that are of high value, are inevitably linked to difficult choices. Those are the choices that will change your life forever. I know so many people who would love to accomplish great things in life, but they have to know, and accept, that they need to make some tough choices in order to get to where they want to be in life.

How many of you right now, today, are willing to make those difficult choices, and follow through with the hard work of those choices that will reward you for the next five or ten years?

God will surely place the right people in my path to help me find the opportunities that I need that will take my life where it needs to be. It hasn't been easy and I didn't expect it to be so. I truly believe that some of our greatest accomplishments will be the result of our toughest and most righteous choices in life and I'm living proof of that. Sometimes the choices can be life-changing because they often determine who we are as a person and can leave us with more meaningful learning experiences.

EIGHT

THE LOVE STORY THAT STARTED IT ALL

What so many misunderstand about love..is its power to heal . . . If one will allow it too. Love is made up of the most potent and deliciously intense ingredients. It can withstand the test of time, and weather any storm. Love can damage any walls built to block its entrance. It has the power to change everything. No matter how confused, drained, sad, angry, or defiant you are, love will win you over at the drop of a dime. There are so many aspects of love . . . but there is one kind of love that can't be matched, copied, tricked, forgotten, or undone. That is a love that is true. A love ordained by God before we ever even enter this earth.

CAME TO THE UNITED STATES in March of 2015. I had a friend from Haiti that was living here and his family let me live with them. Though it was nice to be with people I knew, it just didn't quite feel right, and I decided to make a change with faith. At the time, I was attending church with other single young adults in the area, and one of them, Eric, had become my friend. He invited me to stay on his couch until I could find a more permanent situation. I gratefully accepted.

One night a girl named Melissa invited me, Eric, and his other two roommates to a cookie party at her house. I didn't really know what this meant, but I went. Up to this point, things had been somewhat challenging for me. People couldn't understand me very well. I had to repeat myself over and over until they got what I was trying to say. Others didn't trust me just because of my outward appearance. I really didn't feel too close to many people, other than my roommates.

But then, at the cookie party, as I sat on my own in the corner of the room, a beautiful girl with blond hair walked toward me. She had a sincere smile on her face and she just started talking to me, with no hesitation.

"Hey," she said, "you must be Williamson."

"Yes, that's me."

"I heard that you're living with Eric. I'm Sharla."

I smiled up at her. "It's nice to meet you, Sharla."

"Tell me about you," she said.

From the first moment I met her I was astounded at how sincerely interested she was in getting to know me. She didn't seem scared of me, or suspicious of me in any way, and she seemed to understand my English just fine. Talking to her made me feel happy, like someone was finally looking at the real me. Someone was interested in getting to know the real me. Sharla wasn't asking me questions to judge me for my answers. She genuinely wanted to hear what I had to say.

I told her everything about me. I told her why I was in the U.S., what I was working toward, what I wanted in life, my goals, my dreams. She was very easy to talk to. But I wanted to know about her, too. She was a teacher, she had her own goals and dreams in life, and she was very determined. She had served a mission for our church and she seemed to love the Gospel as much as I did.

"Sharla, do you love the temple?" I asked her at one point during our conversation. The temple is a special place that members of our church visit as often as we can.

"Yes, I do," she answered.

"Would you like to go to the temple with me on Thursday?"

"Sure!"

In my head, I had just asked Sharla on our first date. In Sharla's head, I had just asked her for a ride to the temple, because she knew I didn't have a car. So she showed up with her friend Melissa to pick me up the next day. To say I was disappointed would be an understatement!

But we still had a nice time. I learned even more about Sharla, and I really liked everything I learned. I wanted to spend more time with her. So, two days later, I invited her to go for a walk in the park. This time, she was aware it was a date and she left Melissa at home.

I held her hand during that walk, and later found out that it freaked her out a bit! Hand-holding is a little more of a big deal here than it is at home. In Haiti, friends hold hands all the time. Even two men commonly hold hands as they walk. It doesn't mean anything weird, or dramatic. Just friendship. Obviously, I still had a lot to learn at this point.

But Sharla was patient with me and didn't get scared away. A few days later, while we were watching a movie at a theater, she kissed me for the first time. Well, ok, she insists that it was me that kissed her, but we'll just have to agree to disagree on this one.

Many don't know this, but I was so broke —I was cutting trees for a company and I didn't get paid a lot. I had to skip lunch for the entire year so I could save enough to take care of everything that I wanted to do at that time, especially taking her out on dates. Even though she didn't want me to pay for her plate because she knew that I didn't have enough money, I wanted to court her and treat her right. My mother in Haiti would insist on paying for my English test and also my school materials, but that was all the help she could provide coming from a poor country. I wanted to give my future wife and kids a life that neither myself, nor my family ever had. I knew I had to work extra hard here in this country in order for me to be the kind of husband and father that I wanted to be for my wife and for my children.

"Love is patient, love is kind. It does not envy, it does not boast, it is not proud. It does not dishonor others, it is not self-seeking, it is not easily angered, it keeps no record of wrongs."   – 1 COR. **13:3**

Our path after that was tumultuous. Love usually is that way! We had challenges that many others don't have. For one thing, I didn't pass the English test, over and over again, and that meant I had to return to Haiti for a time. For another, many people in Sharla's life weren't happy that she was dating me. I was different in every way possible. I was black. I was an immigrant from Haiti. I didn't speak English well. I didn't have a good job or a car. I wasn't going to school at that time. There were many reasons why they were against our relationship from the very beginning. And they were right about those things! Those were my weaknesses at the time. But I also knew that those things didn't define me.

They inspired me to focus more on myself and things I could control, which at that time were my school and my spirituality.

Sharla was torn, divided between her feelings for me and her respect for the feelings of her loved ones. She worried about some of the same things they worried about. Sharla broke up with me when I moved back to Haiti. With all of the factors working against us, Sharla wasn't sure about me for a long time.

What I didn't know during this time is that she was working on herself. She was working on cultivating faith and confidence in receiving her own answers, rather than depending on others and caring so much about what others thought of her. She had amazing experiences that led to building up her own character and self-worth. These are things that she would teach me later, and that have come into play heavily in our family life, as well as in our foundation. I'm grateful for these divine insights that she was able to gain, because they led her to opening her heart back up to a life with me.

In February 2016, we finally got back together for good. We started dating very seriously, with the intention of finding out if we would truly make each other happy as husband and wife. In the end, we decided that it was right for us to be together, despite the fact that almost everyone around us (still!) seemed to be against it. We went forward with our personal convictions and answers to our prayers.

It wasn't an easy decision to come to. It wasn't smooth waters and sailing into the sunset together. It was hard. It was one of the most important decisions we would ever make, and so we had to do what Sharla and I knew was right for us, for our lives. We chose each other. And we continue to choose each other, even when the world tries to tell us we should have chosen differently.

She was my best friend before anything and she will always be.

My precious wife and I were married in the Salt Lake City LDS Temple, on October 7th, 2016. It was a beautiful fall day and I will never forget what I felt.

Since our wedding day, my drive to be a better person, a better husband, and now, a better father, has never stopped. Every day, I need to prove to God and myself that I'm working to keep that promise that I made to him to protect, provide for, and cherish my wife. The fact that I had to work so hard for this blessing makes it even more precious to me. If I had a do-over on this life, I would still choose her, even with all the challenges we've faced. I would marry her all over again.

I believe that in its truest essence, love lives inside us. For me, that story holds true. It's become my entire life, every breath I take. A love story that began with some very difficult blocks, has made it as strong as it is today. Love takes work. It isn't easy at all, and the only way you will find your love is when you choose to fight for it. My true love and I had the whole world against us, but we rose above it.

We knew without a shadow of a doubt that we were doing what God wanted, so we jumped in with both feet planted firmly on the ground, never moving or stumbling off course again. We powered through to a win for our love and know that we will be on this journey together for all eternity.

"Love is such a powerful force. It's there for everyone to embrace—the kind of unconditional love for all of humankind. That is the kind of love that impels people to go into the community and try to change conditions for others, to take risks for what they believe in."

– Coretta Scott King

Today, my wife and I stop at nothing to spread that very love amongst the world.

It's amazing how far we can go with our spouse, when we both look to God for counsel, create boundaries, heal our past, focus on ourselves, and the things we can control. Today, my amazing wife and I have three precious children; Tevin, Kai, and Sidonie. We do our very best to live life to the fullest.

NINE

MY HERO'S JOURNEY

My father, Wilson Sintyl, and my mother, Roselaine Florestal Sintyl, have been married for over Thirty-Five years and have paved the way for me to be where I am today. My mom and dad prayed for everything that I have, and everything that I am today.

MY FATHER'S UNWAVERING FAITH while I was under that building has remained an inspiration to me. A fathers love is immeasurable, and his willingness to do absolutely anything to get me out still pierces my heart to this very day. The moment the orphanage collapsed, and my Dad realized that the orphans and I were all under that three-story building, it was like a match had lit inside of him. While trying to keep himself from completely falling apart, he jumped to action; yelling and gathering friends to help him get us out.

He gave more than 120 percent of himself and never once lost faith that a miracle would take place. He knew that somehow, heaven would open and do something about the situation. My dad's faith was unshakeable and he knew and felt something that nobody else did. Dad has always been my hero. I can't say enough about the great man that he is, and all of the ways in which he has been an example to me in my life. But sharing his story has been hard for me, because of all the tough experiences he went through trying to become somebody. I want to do him justice.

When my siblings and I were growing up, he would always tell us to stay in school because education has always been, and always will be, the greatest investment any of us could make. When my dad was young, he started his education later than most. His parents (my grandparents) had never attended school, but were determined that their children would. They were willing to **sacrifice** everything they had, sell anything they could, to send even one child to school.

They lived in a very rural part of Haiti that was very poor and most people received just enough money to live from the crops they grew. They didn't have the money to send all four, so they had a hard decision to make: which of their four children would they send?

After much thought and reflection, they chose my dad, **Wilson**. It wasn't an easy decision, and it certainly wasn't easy for them to see the other three children who couldn't go with Wilson to also receive education. But they made the decision they thought was best.

In 1984, modern modes of transportation

weren't available to them, so they had to use their animals to take them where they needed to go. Wilson's family only had one animal, they used it to take their goods to the public market. This meant my dad had to walk to school.

Every day he walked four hours round-trip, occasionally staying with someone closer to the school, and only coming home on weekends. At times he didn't know if he would have anything to eat when he stayed with his parents' friends, but school was more important than anything to him.

He worked so hard that he got the highest scores in the school. As a result, the director of the department in Saint-Michel de l'Attalaye public school was impressed and took notice of Wilson. He and others met with Wilson's parents about permitting their other children to come to school for free. Because of his hard work and determination, Wilson and all of his siblings were able to get a free education.

I can only imagine my dad's great joy at the realization that his sacrifice was making this possible for his family. How proud my grandparents must have been! But this also pushed my dad to work even harder. Their futures at that school still depended on him and his hard work and dedication. In the end, all four of them graduated from high school, fulfilling their parents' dreams.

When my father graduated from high school, he decided to move to Port-au-Prince, Haiti from St Michel de l'Attalaye (177 kilometers away, or over 110 miles). That's where he started college, at the State University of Haiti in 1989. The State University of Haiti was one of Haiti's most prestigious institutions of higher education at that time.

We all have big dreams resting on our shoulders, and we must carry them with confidence and dignity. There are millions of people who are counting on our efforts in order to help change their own lives. I don't know what would have happened if my grandparents had chosen one of his other siblings instead of my dad.

What I do know is that my dad was born for greatness, and he was given the opportunity to help change his siblings' lives for the better. As he gets older, he continues to dedicate his life to help children in the street, single mothers, and unprivileged families across Haiti. He founded 5 public schools and a couple of orphanages to support Haitians.

My Dad has always been my mentor and inspiration. I remember growing up, he would always get up around 3 or 4 AM because he was so determined to do great things. He never stopped looking for ways to serve his community. Everyone who knows my dad knows how hard he has worked to get where he is now. I know dozens of people who, like me, look up to my Dad as their role model.

I'm grateful for my heroes, my parents. There are so many days where I wish I lived close to them to learn from them. My parents are the definition of resilience and I can't thank them enough for what they've done for me. They gave me life. They love God. They placed education as the center of my life. They lead with dignity, love and compassion.

My precious mother

There is one wonderful soul who has made it possible for me to be here today and it's my precious mom, Roselaine. My mom has always been the bridge to get me anywhere. She has been through a lot in her short life. She has a deep faith in God that has carried my family through many hard things. My mom has something special about her that I can't really describe.

One of my best decisions was to serve a full time mission for my church and I remember how hard that decision was to make. The cost to prepare myself with medical checkups and the supplies I needed to prepare me to be a missionary was almost impossible. When I talked to my Dad about it, he wanted to make sure that I could study in college at the same time while I was serving a mission. I explained to him that wouldn't be possible.

In my country, every year parents go to any length to see if, by a miracle, they can be granted a student scholarship for their kid to study outside the country. That year my dad was granted a full-ride scholarship for me to study in Cuba. He didn't want me to miss that opportunity to study abroad. He told me he would support me only if I could study at the same time.

I remember talking to my mom about the desire to serve and she already knew that a mission was something that I wanted. She was willing to do anything to help me get there. She ended up selling everything she had so that I could have the financial support

I needed to serve a mission for my church. It was tough on her because she had more children and financing a service mission would not have any return on her money. She had faith, even though she wasn't even a member of my congregation at that time, but she knew it was a desire of my heart. There are things in life that will cost you everything; but those things will bring you everything you dreamed of. My missionary service was one of them.

My mother's failing health

My mom is a wonderful woman and I pray daily for my kids, my daughters especially, to be just like her. My mom's parents died when she was 4 years old. At that age, she was just starting to understand what it is like to swim at the big local river called *LaCul* in the south of Haiti. She grew up in the most fruitful neighborhood called *Nan Gwayav* full of fruits with rivers running all over.

That place was magic and carries important meaning to her. Growing up, she had to be raised by her uncle and auntie who were both coming in and out of Haiti to New York. She managed to do all she could to be responsible while staying with cousins in the village. She has so many cousins that she connected with on a deeper level and that she has experienced so many great adventures with. From swimming at the river every day, selling their fruits and products at the local street market, riding bicycles and motorcycles, to attending school together, they had a good simple life.

When she turned 24, she and 2 of her siblings decided to pursue a different path in Port-au-Prince. She moved to the capital to look for better job opportunities after getting an Associate in Public Health Care in Les Cayes Community College in 1986.

She found a job at the government in Haiti in the Health department and has been working there since as a supervisor for the nurses and maintenance crew. That's where she met my Dad while he was also working for the Haiti Health department as an Accountant. The two decided to build a life together that would take them on a journey to buy blocks, concrete and cement to build their first house together in Bicentenaire, Port-au-Prince where they would raise me and my other siblings.

A couple of years after I was married, my wife and I were living in Salt Lake City and we had a one-year-old. I was a tired father working hard and trying to make ends meet. I was on my way home from work one day and I got an unexpected call from my fifteen-year-old sister Wilkerline who lived in Haiti with my mom. She was crying and sounded very scared. The only thing I understood from her words were the words "Manman mouri" or in English "Mom died." My mom was only 49 at the time and those were the last words I wanted to hear from my sister. I pulled my car over on the freeway and my heart broke into a million pieces. I could barely get my body to breathe.

A few moments later my sister called back to inform me that mom had collapsed in the hospital while at work with my sister by her side. But after a few moments, she became coherent and opened her eyes. What my sister thought was dead, was actually a major stroke. For the first few days she couldn't walk, talk, or feed herself. She was basically a vegetable, had lost the mobility on the whole right side of her body. We knew that Haiti didn't have the right tools to help her heal from her stroke. Therapy in Haiti is so hard to find. That night, I went to bed praying for miracles and seeking guidance on what we should do next so we can save her life. In the middle of the night, my wife and I made the decision to bring my mom to Utah with my two fifteen-year-old twin siblings. It was a hard and complex decision but the life of my mother was too precious to risk. Seven days after her stroke my mom and my two siblings boarded a plane to come to Salt Lake City.

After they arrived in Utah, we didn't really know how everything would work out but we trusted that God would provide. A wonderful family that welcomed me to their home when I moved to Utah in 2015 accepted to have my two youngest siblings stay at their place while attending high school in the area.

As we searched for help for my mother people started coming into our lives. The money to get them here immediately was a lot because flights were expensive. A gentleman who didn't even know us messaged us over Facebook and donated all the money needed to cover the flights and some medical equipment. We knew God was aware of us and especially my mom, Roselaine.

We had an occupational therapist and a speech therapist both volunteer their time and they would come to our house to work with my mother. My wife's family knew a doctor who worked with stroke patients at the University of Utah hospital and after going to see him once, he offered to come to our house for future visits so we wouldn't have to pay anything for further visits. He got us on all the right medications to help her start to heal.

When we went to intensive physical therapy many therapists would end up donating their time to us after hearing about my mother's story. The miracles that came to us were immeasurable and she began to heal. When she arrived in Utah she couldn't stand by herself or even talk. Six months later when she went back to Haiti she was able to walk without a cane and speak normally. My siblings decided to stay in Utah and finish high school. They did so well and worked hard in school. They are now attending college and I am so proud of the people they have become.

My mother has always been my hero and having a stroke was the trial of her life. She was so independent and always working hard and much of that independence was taken from her when she had a stroke. Through determination and hard work she was able to overcome many of the effects of that.

She would wake up every morning and push even harder than the day before in all of her exercises she had to do. Having her in our home was such a blessing and the way she was able to bond with my firstborn and my wife was a huge bonus. One other huge bonus was the day she told us she wanted to be baptized. My whole life she had never committed to the church but after her life was spared from the stroke she felt it was God giving her another chance. I was able to baptize her in November 2018, just two months after her stroke, and it was a full-circle moment and one that I had been praying for for a long time.

This whole stroke experience was just another testament to me of one more way that God had helped use me to serve him and his beautiful children, just like I had promised him while I was under the rubble for twenty-eight hours.

Counting my blessings

I had the greatest opportunity growing up to be raised by amazing parents who not only guided me in the right direction, but believed that education, confidence, and a good attitude toward life, were crucial.

My mom would wake us up at 6:00 AM every day to help us get ready for school, and would drop us off there at 7:00, before the national hymn would signal the beginning of school at 8:00. I remember days when I didn't want to leave my mom to go to school. I was very attached to my family, but that's pretty normal in a country like Haiti.

A picture of light, resilience, and strength.
My parents are truly my Heroes! They prayed for
years for the life I have today and I bless their name.
My Mom (53) and Dad (58).

When school was over for the summer, I would either go to Les Cayes, the province where my mother came from, the South part of Haiti or Saint-Michel de L'Attalaye where my dad came from, to spend time with my extended family. I learned how to swim and cook, ate lots of fruit, and connected with my cousins during those summers. These areas of Haiti and these memories hold a special place in my heart.

Today, I am grateful that I was born in Haiti. Here are some of the things I learned while growing up there:

- Appreciate the simple things
- Fight hard, even if it's just to survive another day
- Endure to the end
- Work hard to accomplish things others might think are impossible
- Keep my eyes open and my mouth closed in dangerous situations
- Work hard in school because that is the ticket to success
- How to have resilience even when the storms of life seem never-ending

- How to have absolute faith even when I lost everything I owned
- The value of my own life
- The value of mothers, because "manmanm se pi gwo trezò mwen" or "My mom is my greatest treasure"
- Share, even if there is not enough for me
- Think bigger
- Be resourceful and make something out of nothing
- Believe in myself, even when hope seems lost. Focus on the things I can control in my own environment
- Haitians are a powerful people and Haiti will change someday

I will never be embarrassed that I was born in Haiti. I learned life in a different way. What I have lived, what I have seen, and what I understand helps me appreciate life more. Because I grew up in Haiti, I am the person I am today.

I will never forget Haiti. I will do everything I can to help Haiti become the country we all want to see, to inspire Haitians to believe in themselves, create their best lives, and impact their communities for good. I am fighting to make my country better than it was. This will be my way of showing my gratitude for the land of my ancestors.

As a child who was born in Haiti, I believe that I have something special to contribute somehow to help rebuild this country. Growing up, I've always wanted to help spark a change in Haiti. I believe that my origin is my identity and that's something I cannot change but I will do all I can to change the reality of where I came from.

TEN

I AM A SURVIVOR

The key to being a survivor is knowing your WHY. Power comes in knowing the why behind your reason to live another day, but also learning the power that comes from knowing where you come from and who you are.

THE EARTHQUAKE EXPERIENCE would have broken me more if I didn't realize that it made me who I am today. What most people don't know is that I only have one solid reliable arm from the experience in 2010. My two wrists were broken and one is still struggling to get normal strength, my back has many small scars, and my right knee is not always as strong as it should be.

After about 20 hours stuck in the building, my father could finally hear me. He could hear my voice. He knew I was alive. It took another eight agonizing hours, during which I nearly let go. I was severely parched, I was in pain, and I was hungry. I'd lost all the contents from my stomach, which were smeared on my face. I'd listened as twelve children's cries and screams faded, and I was in anguish at the thought of those children, all dead. I felt almost detached from my broken body and mind. I felt that at any second, I could drift away, to the next life, to the big mystery of whatever comes after death.

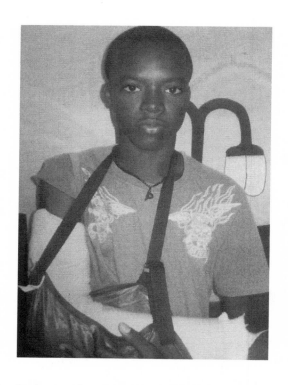

My dad was desperately rallying any strong workers from the streets that he could. He was offering money or anything they wanted to help get me out. My dad is a man that is very small in stature and in strength and he knew he couldn't do it alone. The people he convinced to come help him had to give up on finding their own loved ones to help get me out. It took a whole team of people. Imagine trying to dig through big walls of concrete with only your bare hands and maybe a pick. They would have to drive the pick in the concrete to make small cracks. They could only hammer that pick for so long before they needed a break and the next worker would start hammering while others would drag big blocks of concrete to the side.

After each aftershock, everyone helping my dad would leave to go check on their family and friends again and my dad had to start over to find more workers to continue the rescue attempts to get me out. When they started getting closer in the last few hours the whole team only had three picks that they were using to break these concrete blocks. I could hear them asking for a break each time as they're chipping away at every piece of concrete that was on top to get them to where I actually was. They put in hours and hours of cramping arms and tired backs under the hot sun working to save this man's son. They were determined to do what it took to get me out.

My dad's very important mission was to motivate them and remind them that his son is under the building and that I'm still alive. It had gotten to a point where people were only focusing on those that were still alive and calling for help. For some, it was impossible because I was too far from the surface of the rubble but my Dad knew something that they didn't know and felt something they didn't feel.

It wasn't easy for me and TiBlanc under the building, either. A sweet, intelligent, little boy named Samdi, who was also TiBlanc's little cousin in the orphanage, was among the other eleven children that were stuck not too far from where we were. TiBlanc and Samdi were best friends. They were the only family they had there in the orphanage and they were basically like brothers. TiBlanc would occasionally call on Samdi to make sure that he was okay but Samdi started losing his voice like the others, until we couldn't hear him anymore and that's when I knew that he was gone.

TiBlanc knew something was wrong at the moment but continued to stay hopeful that he would be able to make it. I can imagine what he was thinking underneath me during that time. I'm sure his little heart was breaking but he didn't mutter a word about it under the rubble. He knew our focus was to save ourselves and if we were able to do only that then it would be a complete miracle.

When the team led by my father finally got down closer to us they sent a man down the hole that they had dug to come get us and he got stuck. So they worked for a while longer to get him out first. Then they sent him down again with a long rope to wrap around my neck so they could pull me out. I finally managed to move enough to get the rope around my neck and they started pulling. My limbs were all numb of course and when they started pulling I realized that my body was not going to budge because of the big block that was on my right arm, crushing it.

I yelled to them to explain what was going on and after a long pause they yelled back and told me they would have to make a different hole through a different part of the building to get my arm unstuck first. I knew that would take much longer but there was no other way. It was disappointing and definitely a set-back but I hoped that it would lead to freedom.

After more hours of waiting they started getting close to my arm and were able to successfully remove enough weight off of it to get it free. Then they pulled the rope again and drug me out. The light of day was so blinding but so refreshing. There were many moments under the rubble that I didn't know if I would ever see the light of day again. I WAS FREE!

As soon as they carried me out, I remember so much water. I drank and they poured it all over me. Gallons and gallons of water. I couldn't stand or walk on my own, so they took me to the Protestant church sanctuary while digging TiBlanc out, and I slept and slept. The pain was unbearable as my limbs started gaining feeling again. I could feel every small scratch, deep wound and broken bone that had been numb for almost the whole time I was under the rubble.

TiBlanc and I went to two different camp-sites because his parents took him back to Jeremie, south of Haiti. I heard that after Ti-Blanc came out he kept asking about Samdi. But they all knew that Samdi had already passed.

I had a strong connection with TiBlanc before the earthquake. We shared many tasks together while I was in charge of taking care of these chores. He was my supporter and under my care at the orphanage. He would help me with anything I needed help with and was like a little brother to me. After the tragedy, my love for him grew and still grows. To see him go back home right after that tragedy was a heart-breaking moment. But I knew that God would continue to watch over him like He did to me.

If not for TiBlanc, I wouldn't be here. Every time my body tried to let go, I remembered the boy trapped underneath me. I needed to stay alive for him. I told him we would live, and so we had to live. But most importantly, I'd made a promise to God. And I intended to keep that promise.

"Williamson, are we going to die?"

I said, "No, we're not. We're going to live."

Twenty-eight hours after the shaking started under our feet, TiBlanc and I emerged from the rubble. Many have asked me, "Where is TiBlanc, Williamson?"

Several years after the earthquake, I tried to reach out to TiBlanc to reconnect with him but his family had a different idea about that. They thought I was going to use him for something and they didn't allow me to reconnect with him without giving them something in return. I wish he could be a part of this book and share his own memories of being buried under that building together during these twenty eight hours. I know he will read this story that you are reading now. Eventually in his own language. He is the only person in the world who truly knows how hard, miserable, and tough it was for us and also the other children from the orphanage that died.

I didn't see my mom until the day after I was rescued.

She ran into the church screaming. "My boy, you're alive! You're alive!" She cried as she knelt next to me, laid her head on my chest, and sobbed, great heaving sobs that racked her whole body. She kept touching my face and hands as if to make sure I was actually there.

I would not have lived if she hadn't come to pick me up that day. All at once, I felt something like loneliness, though that didn't make sense to me because I was surrounded by people. But I felt alone, knowing that all of my classmates were gone. They didn't exist on the earth anymore. I was the only one.

It was at that moment that I realized I must have been saved for a purpose. I should have been one of them, but I wasn't. My mom shouldn't have come to get me that day, but she did. I should have died with all the rest of the kids in the orphanage, but I didn't.

Why?

That was the question that wracked my soul from that moment on. Why me? Why was I spared? Why did God see fit to save me and only me from among my classmates? Was it because I was the class president? I was a leader in life and I had to keep being the leader with all this death around me?

But why?

I couldn't get them out of my head. For months I couldn't walk. I lay in my tent, unable to get up, when all I wanted was to go and see my school. I wanted to help find them, but at the same time, I didn't want to see them. I wanted to pay my respects at their final resting place, but I hated the thought of it at the same time.

My mind was occupied with memories of my classmates from my school. The memory of who they used to be.

Lucien. He was a skinny, humble kid. He didn't talk much, but was very smart and wanted to be a doctor. Now he would never be a doctor.

Richkard. He taught me how to write with beautiful handwriting. He loved to draw. He didn't do well on tests and other assignments, but he would draw buildings and other amazing designs. He wanted to be an architect. Now he would never be an architect.

Louis. He wanted to be a pastor, because his dad was a pastor. Now he would never be a pastor.

But most of all, I thought about my best friend, Benson. He was very sure of himself. He had major swagger, and was sure all the ladies were after him. On the Day of Color, flag day in Haiti, we would wear our best clothes because it was the only day of the year we didn't have to wear our blue and pink uniforms. We'd perform our beats for the talent show and he would go all out. I laugh just thinking about it.

It is one thing to be a victim of this terrible earthquake that shook my homeland. It is another thing to be a survivor. According to the Oxford Dictionary, a victim is, "a person harmed, injured, or killed as a result of a crime, accident, or other events or actions." One of the definitions of survivor is, "a person who copes well with difficulties in their life."

The difference is very small and subtle, yet incredibly profound. That small difference between being a victim and being a survivor is simply a choice. The definition of victim is very broad and includes anyone involved in a number or events. But to become a survivor, one must cope well, which is done with the choices we make. That first choice can come at any point after the event that made them a victim and affects every single decision that comes later with a long-lasting impact.

I had been through a very rough experience that, luckily, many will not have to go through. I could easily have cried about how much I had lost and how difficult it was. However, I knew I was saved for a purpose. I chose to focus on the future and what I could build, and who I could become.

In order to rise from the rubble in our lives, we have to let go of the rubble. We can't cling to it, stay in it, and define ourselves by this experience. I had to move past the experience of the earthquake.

I obviously have not forgotten about the experience. That is also something completely different. I can remember what happened and the profound experiences that have taught me so much. I can remember the blessings I received. I can even remember the hard parts. But when I think of that day, I share what I have learned and how I have grown. I do not share the story so that people will feel sorry for me. I do not share as an excuse as to why I cannot do something.

I share my purpose and the promise I made to God to empower others—to help them rise as I have risen from the debris of that building. I rose and stepped away, moving forward with my life. Yes, there was sadness and desolation all around me, but it makes my purpose that much easier. When we hit rock bottom, the only direction to go is up. I could do more, take risks, learn, and study because things could only get better.

My Own Self

I learned a long time ago the wisest thing I can do is be an advocate for myself, for young people and others like me. I chose to cheer myself on. I chose to work for a better future. Sitting in that tent, I knew I wouldn't be here long. I knew I wouldn't be one who simply took the handouts given. I had, and still have, a promise to fulfill. I have important work to do.

When we are at our lowest point, it can be so difficult to see the world in any other way. Grief can be all-consuming. I had lost so much during that earthquake, but I had the choice to be bitter about losing my friends and my home, or I could look at what I could do in the circumstances I was in. I could constantly wish I had things the way they used to be, or I could build something greater.

When that building fell around me, it may not seem like an act of creation. But as we cleared away the debris, what was left over? Some would say nothing while others would say there was space created. The land that housed an orphanage could now be like a blank canvas where we could create anything that we wanted. We could build a new, better orphanage. We could build a park. We could build a church. We could build a home.

Often when we lose something, we focus so much on the loss that we forget to see the opportunities that come with it. Yes, I lost my home, but I have found a new home with my wife and my own children. Yes, I lost many friends. I think about them often and honor their memory as I make new friends and build a life they would have been proud of.

I had to choose to believe in myself and trust myself. It doesn't matter how anyone else views us in these situations. There may have been many who would simply have seen me as a victim of a tragic accident, gave me a few handouts, and went on their way. The Bible teaches us in Ecclesiastes 3:4 that there is, "A time to weep, and a time to laugh; a time to mourn, and a time to dance."

I do not want to make it sound like we are not allowed to mourn and grieve when we lose someone important to us. If we do not grieve, we do not heal. If we really want to make a difference in this life, we have to be able to give the best of ourselves. Only God and our own self knows what we need and what is best. The higher we rise, the more others will try to tell us who we are. They will tell you that you aren't good enough. You don't know what you are doing. It's a pointless endeavor. They might even try to call you things like liar, worthless, rude, and more.

This is another reason we need to have the divine on our side. We need to know and understand our true worth so we can stand up for ourselves. As we keep our principles in place, we can also advocate for others. We first need to know that whatever comes our way, we are not merely victims, we are survivors. We can face whatever comes our way and continue to rise.

This is real success. To be successful, we continue to rise by coping with anything that happens and rising higher because of it. Success comes to us when we are doing our best in God's eyes and in our eyes. There are enough people in the world who will see your efforts and choose to stand with you and rise with you.

Courage

In order to be a survivor, and rise from our rubble, we need to have courage. It is not easy to face anything and everything that life and other people throw at us. Anyone can be a victim, not everyone is a survivor. Being a survivor is more, and requires us to rise to a higher level. Just because we are currently trapped in rubble, doesn't mean we have to stay there.

I was trapped under that building for twenty-eight hours. That was a physical entrapment. Once I was physically free from the bricks and stones, doesn't mean I was automatically emotionally released from the experience. I had to make that choice to not remain stuck in the rubble of my emotions. No matter what the situation is, it is easy to feel stuck. But that is not true. We are never stuck in a situation, in a job, in a relationship, or anything else. We always have the option to rise, if we have the courage.

It takes courage to stand and advocate for yourself and others. It takes courage to dream that life could be different or better. No matter how grim life feels, in fact, especially at those lowest moments, the only way to go is up. It can seem impossible. You may think you don't have the ability; but the only ability you need is courage.

Victors

While being a survivor is a great thing, even more important is knowing that there is a step above. We can become more than survivors; we can become victors. Haitians are known for their resilience. This is a great word. I'm proud of my people for having this very important trait.

In the United States, people work for a new home, a new car, a new computer, or other things. Haitians work to survive on just two dollars per day. Getting out of survival mode as a Haitian takes privilege or a lot of tenacity and hard work.

I wish we as Haitians were known for so much more. I have seen so much of what Haitians are capable of. I want us to be known as creators, peacemakers, resourceful, and more. Moving from the victim mindset to the survivor mindset is a huge success. It takes another huge mindset shift to move from survivor to victor. Each person has the ability to make a name for themselves and to achieve success. We are all capable of doing great things to make the world a better place. Both the world around us and our own individual world.

Similar to moving from victim to survivor, the shift into becoming a victor is a choice in our mindset. When we choose to learn and grow from the experience, we are taking it as a tool into our hands for us to shape our future. We choose to forgive, to let go, and our emotions take directions from our thoughts. Choosing the better thought will lead us to better actions. It means we get to upgrade. Talking about victim, survivor, and victor, we can also think of it in terms of "Good, Better, Best."

Even as a victim, we are living beings with value. We have good traits and are still good people trying our best. This is good. But then when we choose to shift into survivor mode, we get better. We start to see more success and see the things we can accomplish and are more aware of others. From there, we shift into the best version of ourselves. The version God meant for us to become. We become victors.

It is hard to be a survivor. It is no small feat to move to this level of living. It shows how powerful you can be when we have to be. We can take those same lessons and experiences, put forth that power and energy to succeed, even when it feels less necessary. I still work like my life depends on it. My life as I know it and as I want it to be does depend on it. If I want to own a house, I work like my life depends on it, because the life I want depends on me owning that house.

A vital principle we can learn in hard times is how incredibly powerful we can be. When we have to be, we are able to accomplish incredible feats. I never would have thought it was possible to survive under the crushing weight of a three story building without food or water for twenty eight hours. Yet, it had been done. I did it. Even though there were many times I didn't think I would make it any longer. It isn't just me, either. There are many incredible stories of surviving against the odds.

Surviving also taught me many principles on how to get what I wanted. A victor mentality has helped me stay above the darkness of my past experiences. I do not fall back underneath the rubble of my yesterday, but instead, move forward to tomorrow. I move forward because I know the best is yet to come. Keep going!

Success

Often we think we can jump straight to success after adversity. However, life doesn't work that way. After the earthquake, I had to become a survivor. Once I managed that, I could move on to the next level of success. The next level can be many things including a new job, deeper relationships, seeking education and more. For me, that was moving to the United States. Once in the States I had to start over, again. I was again surviving before I could gain success.

When I first came to Utah from Haiti, it was a struggle to survive. I had to work so hard. Having no friends or family, I had to find a place to stay and I had to find a way to eat. I still had to have my basic needs met, but was trying to do so in a country where I didn't speak the language. Once I found the basics, I had to keep that going while I figured out how to speak English, and do it well enough to be understood.

Being a survivor has brought out the best part of me. It brought out my ability to discover more. Because I know I am capable of doing hard things, I am able to keep going just a little longer. Like when I moved to Utah and had to pass an English test. I failed that test five times. Five times I was told I wasn't good enough. Yet, I kept practicing.

It may seem like a small thing, but it was my smile that helped me to survive. Not only because it kept my spirits up, but also because I could serve people in this way. When I saw someone was feeling sad, I would come over, wrap my arm around them, and smile. Something as small as a smile can really impact others around me. They knew I was friendly and well-meaning.

My smile reminded me that I was doing great things and reminded me to stay. I wasn't any less, I was surviving in a new environment. I could go back home, but I would spend the rest of my life playing it comfortably. I also knew I had promises to keep. I kept trying.

I kept attending church activities, even when I was tired and didn't feel like it. I was willing to spend time trying to connect with others and use the time as well as practice my English. Each time I failed the test, I knew it wasn't really a failure. Each of these failures were actually opportunities. They were opportunities to practice more and become better. They were opportunities to learn. And learning helps me to survive another day.

This is what brings true success. Doing what you can, then doing just a little more more, a little bit better. When we gain success, we become more than what we were before, and can move to the next level. But moving to the next level is making sure that we can first survive on that level, then learn to thrive and have success.

In psychology, there is a concept pyramid called Maslow's Hierarchy of Needs. In this pyramid, there are five levels—Physiological needs, Safety needs, Love & belonging, Esteem, and Self-actualization. This pyramid is not something that we simply rise through just once. We start over in each new situation, rising through each level in a new context. After the earthquake in Haiti, I learned how to survive there, learned how to live my life in a new way. I went through this Hierarchy of Needs there. Then I came to Utah and had to start all over. I started this process over as I began married life with my sweet wife, as I started running my nonprofit **Arise Project for Humanity**, and again as I moved to Georgia. Each level takes me from a survivor to a champion.

It gives me the confidence to keep going when things get difficult. I survived an earthquake that killed over 250,000 people. I can survive anything. I survived coming to Utah and living in a country where I didn't know the language. I can survive anything. I have created a family, a business, survived being alone, going to school, and instilled love for my fellow men deep into my heart.

Creators

Moving up through each level of this pyramid requires a new mindset shift. And each new level is something we are able to create through our mastery of the level that came before. We have incredible power and ability to create each new level of our life. We are creators. We are designed to create. It may be creation through artistic means such as paintings, music, or books, but it might not be.

We are creators in every conversation we have, in every choice we make, and in every action we do. Even more so as survivors. I recognize that if I had not lived through this earthquake, I would have been unable to create a lot of things. As we survive, we are able to create good things that go out into the world and make it a better place. The better we become at creating things that uplift and inspire others, the more we continue on our path to becoming victors.

We always have the choice to elevate our words, our thoughts, and our actions to make them rise to a level above. As we do that, we rise as well. What do you want to create? What is your next step that would lead you towards creating this?

ELEVEN

GIVING BACK TO THE LAND

I can't think of a better way to leave my mark in the world, than by empowering my Haitian people and those in the Caribbean to rise up and be the maker of their own destiny. From the beginning, I knew that I was saved for something greater. Something that has to do with my home country. It's my honor to be a part of the change we all want to see in **Haiti.**

No MATTER WHAT MISSION you are on in life, there will always be people that you are meant to help and to serve. The principles will be the same, no matter who you are helping. For me, this meant giving back to the land that I came from.

Some of the issues Haiti faced prior to the 2010 earthquake persist today, including weak political governance, lack of infrastructure, and limited access to basic resources. Haiti ranks among the world's least developed countries because of political, social, and environmental insecurity. The earthquake registered at a high level impact magnitude of 7.0. That's a high level of energy, and because it occurred at 6.2 miles below the surface, a shallow depth, its powerful energy had a devastating effect at ground level.

The epicenter of the 2010 quake was near Port-au-Prince, the capital city, with more than 2 million people in the metropolitan area. Many of Port-au-Prince's multi-story concrete buildings collapsed in a deadly heap, because they were poorly constructed. There were no building codes enforced.

One of our trips to Haiti with a group of volunteers from Utah to help train our new mentors from the Mentoring Program in St Marc, Haiti. We have traveled with them to Port-au-Prince, Les Cayes, Deschapelles, Montrouis, Archahaie and St Marc.

Recurring disasters, such as Hurricane Matthew in 2016 and the 2021 earthquake also make it hard for Haitian families to overcome entrenched poverty. I've always wanted to do something for my hometown in Haiti. I want to somehow give back. Thoughts and questions of how much good has been done in Haiti, continue to fill my mind. What can

I do that is good, that will last long term? When I started the Arise project, six years ago, it wasn't because I wanted to create something good for myself. It wasn't just because Williamson wanted to help Haiti.

There was much more to it than my own desires. It was because I knew I was alive for a reason. I knew that the promise I made to serve God was also a promise to serve His people. The more I came to terms with the promise I made to God, the more my heart was drawn toward serving my people; the Haitian people.

This mission is about what I can give to others, not what I get in any form. What really matters is that my people are able to receive the help they need, and to receive it in a way that will help them for generations to come. It is more than just having their immediate needs met. While those immediate needs are important, there are things much greater in store for them. We have to make sure we are helping them to meet their own needs, rather than teaching them to rely on others.

I want Haitians to learn to rely on each other, to have a sense of loyalty, comradery, fellowship, and unity among the people. I feel this has been stripped of their souls. There's a deep inner wounding that has been created amongst the land. Those wounds go back many, many generations. Foundations of lack, mistrust, hurt, anger, and pain have been deeply rooted within Haitians. Providing nurturing care of mentorship, and resourcefulness will begin mending what is lost within.

The Arise project is meant to build from the inside out. It's meant to water the seeds, inside the people, that have been lost. Providing the sustenance they need as well will show them we intend to help them beat the odds. Yes, many organizations will provide things like food and clothes, but Haitians also need something greater. They need something better, something that will help them to provide for themselves in the future. They need mentors. They need people they can look up to. They need guidance from those who will set a positive example for what they can one day become. They need to see proof of the brighter days that are up ahead.

I want them to know that somewhere over the rainbow isn't really far at all. They can reach it. I came from nothing, and I'm trying to help them see what can happen in an instant, a moment of decision that prompts change. They can become anything they want to be, if they put in the work.

As I started to travel back to Haiti visiting my grandparents, friends, and neighbors, I started to realize that many have gotten stuck in survivalism. Devastating natural disasters, and tumultuous leaderships, have left Haitians depleted and dependent. Simply surviving has led many into a non-growth mentality, lacking self-esteem, with no expectations or vision for hope. This is the environment that I was raised and grew up in.

When I came to the United States of America, I saw so many opportunities that allowed my own visions to expand. That's when I knew I had to do something to bring the same to Haiti, my people.

One of the biggest issues that I saw was that Haitians don't celebrate each other's success. I believe the reason behind that is what they don't see in themselves. They don't see themselves succeeding, so how can they celebrate it for someone else? They don't recognize their own potential, their own worth, and capacity to thrive, beyond their immediate surroundings. Even the children feel like they're not worthy of anything.

These realizations are sad to me, because I know that isn't true. I have experienced what can happen within, if you believe in yourself. I believed that I could achieve great things and was born to succeed.

When you go inside the villages of Haiti's people and speak to them, you can see they all have a profound, wonderfully resourceful, resilient spirit about them. The souls of the Haitian people make up a nation that has the potential to lift themselves out of the murky waters. The uplifting we can begin now, but I believe it will take the younger generation to ensure the foundation we create today remains concrete.

Our rising generation is worthy of our best efforts to support and strengthen them in their journey to become who they are created to be. Working together, celebrating each other's success, ending corruption, focusing on education, and believing in themselves, will bring so much more abundance in their lives.

We decided to build a mentorship curriculum that focuses on building core values. The foundation of our organization's unique purpose, goal, and vision is grounded by these core values. Those values are embraced by our mentors (local leaders) through our mentoring program at, ARISE Project For Humanity. We work with professional mentors, national, international organizations, and business owners to aid our mentors in becoming certified, so they can professionally mentor young people in their community.

The curriculum was built utilizing a combination of principles from different industries to help young people envision change, expand their mindsets, and then take action on those expansions, thus creating a lively impact on the community regardless of their circumstances. Many young Haitians have been orphaned, which makes them vulnerable and victim to opportunistic predators. We mentor victims of sex trafficking, exploitation, and abuse by helping them build back the part of themselves that was lost from trauma. We also help integrate them back into society, with a more victorious state of mind.

I felt that if we created a program centered around self belief, it would teach Haitians and youth around the world how to get rid of doubts, barriers, and blockages that keep them stagnant in the same vicious cycles of sabotage. The change will help build a sustainable future, by empowering perpetual young leaders. The key is to protect the nation of Haiti, keep its children safe, so they can grow fruitfully into a new future.

As I mentioned previously, mentors have been a powerful influence for me. I have worked with many mentors to accomplish the things I knew I needed to do. With their guidance, I've been able to accomplish more than I had ever hoped for.

My intent isn't to show off my achievements, but is meant to show my dedication to God, by keeping the promises I made to him. When we have been blessed, we have an obligation to bless others. Those blessings become a joyous cycle of everlasting good karma. The kind that is passed on and stands strong through the storms of trying times. Each step I've made along my journey, prepared me to walk through doors of opportunity that at times seemed impossible to open. Impossible or not, I opened them. We have to look at things one step at a time.

Just like when I was under the rubble, I took one breath at a time, and survived one moment longer. Each step helps us to rise a little higher. Each step lifts you further from the struggle. Each moment we live we choose to rise by keeping promises, serving others, and giving back to honor those who have helped us successfully climb the mountain. The formula is simple. The follow-through is difficult, but it is true, and worth it.

It was not easy to encourage TiBlanc, when I wanted to give up myself. It was not easy to be pinned in the same position without food or water for over twenty eight hours. Being committed takes a lot of work, but as we rise to a new level, we also receive an even greater level of abundant favor.

I knew the moment I stood up and decided to engage myself in Haiti's rearing, it wasn't going to be easy. So much has happened since I started the Arise project in 2015. Everyday I'm reminded of all the challenges. I don't give up though, and I never will. I will never grow weary, or tired. My endurance will live on until the hearts of Haitians are pieced together in the form of unity.

I remember one of my trips to Haiti in 2019, while I was driving my car to the capital, someone ran into me. The right side of the car was ripped off. Even though I needed the car to get things done, I decided to leave it on the side of the road, and take a motorcycle to our next stop. It was a five-hour trip to a mentoring training session, in Port-au-Prince. Later, a generous friend of mine helped me pay to get my car fixed.

At 5 AM, when the sun hasn't even come out yet, the streets of Port-au-Prince are already busy. However, the streets aren't busy with cars, since income levels in Haiti are still too low to maintain vehicles. (Haiti ranks 200 among 216 countries in the 2015 Gross National Income rankings published by the World Bank—and the colorful tap-taps, or brightly painted vehicles with lots of decoration, remain unaffordable to most of the population.) At this time of the day, streets are filled with people, walking to work or school, starting their long journeys early, so they can arrive on time. In fact, only 26% of Haitians use any motorized vehicle on a regular basis. The remaining 74% either walk where they have to go, or do not travel at all.

All are forced to walk long distances to reach jobs, often slaloming between vendors and vehicles parked on the curb, and yet, the economic opportunities they try to reach after walking one hour, remain quite limited. Especially in comparison to the pool of jobs the urban area of 3.5 million in Port-au-Prince, can offer. On average, an urban resident in Port-au-Prince that commutes by foot can only reach 12% of the jobs within 60 minutes, and this share goes down as one moves away from the city center and toward the outskirts.

Hardships will occur, but can be without a doubt, overcome. I can't give up on my mission to help my wonderful people, so I expect them not to give up either. If we give up, the next generation will suffer and miss the opportunity to finish the work that we have started. I believe it's going to take years to see the change we all want to see among these people, but I do also believe, with all my heart, that it will happen gloriously, and this nation will one day rise above everything.

The Mission of ARISE Project For Humanity

Our mission is to inspire and empower youth all across the globe through mentoring to change their mindset, create their best life, and impact their community. We hope that what we have to offer touches those we reach in such a way that they feel compelled to give back in the same way. All of our partnerships are about aspiring to inspire.

Mentoring Others

I'd like to tell a very inspiring and powerful story about a forty three year old woman named Augustin. Her story certainly describes the impact of our organization here in Haiti. Augustin was a community leader. She died in 2021 of a heart attack. Her heart trouble was not treated in time due to a lack of emergency care professionals. She was one of our first mentors and worked as a mentor in our program, every year until she died.

The Arise team and I miss her everyday. Before coming onboard, Augustin had heard about the mentoring program and followed our progress for a long time. After deciding to take our mentoring training, she became a mentor in Leogane. Her daughter Jennifer, was the only mentee she had during the first three weeks. Later that season, she ended up meeting with twenty-five other mentees from her community in Leogane.

She met with them every week for twelve weeks, to teach them about the mentoring program, and principles of the curriculum.

All twenty-five mentees graduated from the mentoring program; eleven of them were sex trafficking survivors. After graduating from high school and the mentoring program, they all enrolled into college. Two of them have become journalists, three of them became marketing specialists. Another two now have children of their own, and the last three of the mentees are still currently mentors in our Arise community program.

Today, Augustin's daughter Jennifer, has successfully mentored over thirty other mentees in the Leogane chapter of the program.

We are very proud to say that Jennifer has become one of our Region Leaders in the country. She is now leading dozens of other mentors while supervising hundreds of youth in mentoring programs across Mariani, Gressier, Leogane, Grand Goave, Petit-Goave and many more. I'm so grateful for Ms. Augustin's example to Jennifer. Her nurturing mentorship and expert motherhood inspired Jennifer to become not only a mentor for others, but a force for good in the many generations to come.

There's no better person to lift up a group of people than one who comes from the same place in life. Jennifer has done just that for the people in her community. Before we go and help a country, let's first look for the people who are already helping. Who are they? Have they been through the same challenges that the people in that country are going through? Do they really understand the culture and what they really need? Do they understand how to serve them and the best way to empower them?

Sometimes, without realizing it, we can hurt others by simply giving. I feel like there should be a strategic method to giving. There has to be an even give and take. Upon giving, there needs to be a lesson in place in order for someone to effectively receive that gift. If we only give and don't teach how to receive and earn, then we will end up in an endless cycle of just giving forever. If "help" isn't offered in the right way it can crush an economy, and possibly damage an underdeveloped mindset. People need to understand how to receive with grace and gratitude.

The best way is to teach them how to give to themselves. If you give in this way, people will instinctively learn how to build for themselves. It's like the old saying, "Give a man a fish and you feed him for a day. Teach a man to fish and you feed him for a lifetime."

Let's imagine we come into Haiti with a lot of peanut butter in our suitcases to give to the people. The people will take the peanut butter, and use it, but it will quickly run out. What then? Instead of doing that, why not come in to teach them how they can make the peanut butter? Think of the money they will generate, and be able to invest back into their own economy, as opposed to spending and buying outside of Haiti. Creating a culture that can learn to materialize their own resources independently, also builds a sense of pride and confidence within the group.

Giving back to my people while teaching them how to individualize their own needs is what I aim to do. Access to mentoring not only restores hope for a better future, it also reduces the amount of time spent focusing on the bad and wrong things about the country of Haiti. I thank our supporters for giving youth a chance to unlock their potential through mentoring in the Caribbean and around the world.

I started the mentoring program by locating local communities that were doing the same kind of work on the ground. I was looking for young leaders that were already motivated to lead and learn. I taught them basic principles through my curriculum. That helped them believe in themselves, create the life they needed, so they could later impact the community in a stronger and better way.

If you are looking for a way to help a country or community, you can start by finding local people, local projects, local organizations that are involved there. The best way to help is by supporting and sponsoring the efforts they are already trying to build within their own communities. Give them the keys they need in order to open their own doors.

Another way to help is by remembering the source to all our blessings. I truly believe I would never have survived the earthquake or anything else devastating in my life without God's intervention. I recognized this as I was buried and I prayed. I did not survive because of my own strength or cunning abilities to talk my way out of the trouble, and I do not believe it was simply luck either. It was the sheer will of our Lord and Savior, Father God. He had a purpose for me, and He has a purpose for you. The power of prayer is true. I asked for help to survive and I received it.

Before you go to bed tonight, **please keep Haiti in your prayers.** They need it more than ever. It would be even more beneficial, if you choose to make a donation to a local organization that you trust in Haiti. They're desperately in need of your support. The children of Haiti need to be nurtured and empowered more than ever.

It's imperative that we are brave enough to live life according to the dreams we aspire to. We must forge ahead, with a steadfast outlook on the future, without worry of the expectations and opinions of others. Be vigilant, confident, and stand up for what you believe and know is right. When change is required to adjust to a positive and spiritual way of life, there's no time to be reluctant with the way we move.

Receiving Mentoring

Mentoring is not something that is just meant for those in Haiti, I am well aware that mentorship is necessary for everyone. Mentorship is meant to move everyone to the next level. Olympic athletes do not get where they are just because they like sports. Liking the sport is helpful, obviously, but one key factor is the work and training they commit to leading up to the Olympic games. Business owners aren't just lucky, they do research, they study, they test themselves through trial and error, and they apprentice with like minded business owners who came before them.

Growth is challenging. While it is possible to do it on your own, success becomes more obtainable when we are working with someone who can tell us where the common mistakes are, what to watch for, and what works better. I have never written a book before, I could not have done this without the help of others who have. Coming to the United States, I learned English faster by working with others.

The English poet John Donne has said, "No man is an island entirely of itself. Any man's death diminishes me, because I am involved in mankind." When we learn from others, we then have the capability to teach, and the responsibility to then help as well. When we do not learn and help others to learn, we remove a very key component of being human.

Human beings are social creatures and we are naturally interdependent on each other for our survival. The more we gather together to help one another, the closer we get, the more we learn about each other, the more we are able to practice using our spiritual, and natural gifts. Working together means thriving towards a better tomorrow.

What is something that you have always wanted to do? What is one thing that you know will help you rise from your own rubble? I can promise that someone has done it before and can help you to do it. Find a mentor. Let them help you rise.

As you get past the basic survival mode, your next step should be with a coach, advisor, instructor, guide, teacher, or trainer. Any sort of accountability partner that will help ensure that you make it to the very next step. That next step should be the one that takes you straight to your highest potential. Becoming the very best version of yourself should be your main focus at all times.

The little things we do in life matter, because if we work hard, those little things will become great big things. I aim to see this greatness come out of Haiti. I remember when we started 6 years ago, I went down to Haiti so that I could share with them the life principles that changed my own life. Since then, so many mentoring programs across Haiti have been flourishing with hope. More young people have access to positive role models, more dreams are being discovered, improved changes will continue to be implemented, and more opportunities for our youth to become exactly who they were created to be, will open up.

I'm so grateful for our supporters, despite all the darkness that is going on, they still believe that a better Haiti is possible, and choose to stand with ARISE Project For Humanity, to help uplift Haiti. We can't prevent natural disasters from happening in the world, but we can prevent the weakening of our youths' character. We may not know the storm that lies ahead, but we can equip ourselves, our minds, and spirit on how to weather the storm, if and when it comes. Our mentorship program will always do just that. I promise.

How will Haiti change?

Under the best of circumstances, Haiti cannot be changed structurally without some yielding of power by the haves. The rural sector cannot be expected to increase its own productivity without massive, long-term assistance. Corruption, vulnerability to weather disasters, resurgent gang violence, and disproportionate use of force by police against protesters, remain major human rights concerns.

In the 1700's, Haiti was once the wealthiest colony in the New World, today it is the Western Hemisphere's poorest country, with more than half of its population living below the World Bank's poverty line. Foreign intervention, debt, political instability, and circumstances beyond the peoples control, have stymied the Caribbean country's development. About forty percent of the Haitian population has consistent access to electricity; although the Ministry of Public Works estimates that the coverage could be higher when irregular connections are considered. In urban areas, the total electrification rate is 72 percent, but only 15 percent in rural areas.

To create a healthy and thriving society, there must be certain things in place. These are solutions that we work toward and changes that need to be made in Haiti to see these things become a reality:

Trusted leaders in power play a prominent role in keeping the morality of a group, at a healthy and productive flow. Integrity, humility, courage, forgiveness, and the willingness to make sacrifices, are the attributes that every good leader carries. Leaders must not only be educated and experienced, but it is important to be compassionate when adhering to the problems faced by their people. Leaders in government should be strategic in dealing with financial and contractual matters so that the land and its people can live profitably, with no overhanging debt. Transparency in the day to day workings of the country's governance is a key factor. As it allows the people to see that they, along with their input matters. Naturally every good leader promotes peace within his group, not war and strife.

Investing in the education system will undoubtedly rebuild the economy. Education brings a sense of diligence to the students. It challenges the mind to increase its learning capacity. It also builds a healthy sense of competitiveness amongst the children, so each will care to continue leveling up. The more they know, the more they can build upon.

Ensuring that schools are overflowing with enough space and supplies to tend to every child's needs, should be of utmost importance as well. A healthy space full of positive energy sets the tone for the children to create beyond their wildest dreams. Access to **education** alleviates poverty and restores confidence in attaining a bright future. Right now in Haiti, there's no passion in choosing education as a profession. People simply chose teaching because it's a job that can pay bills. I want to change that ideology.

"Education is the most powerful weapon which you can use to change the world."

– Nelson Mandela

We must support quality education in the following ways:

- student tuition
- teacher training and ongoing support
- innovative, high quality classroom materials
- introduction of technology
- health care services
- facility repairs
- entrepreneurship training and support

Emergency resources will remain a necessity, because of the high pre-existing needs in Haiti. This includes food, shelter, hygiene items, cash assistance, tarps, rebuilding supplies, water, PPE and other supplies.

Health and psychological care are desperately on all levels. Many of the victims of the 2021 earthquake also lived through the 2010 earthquake and Hurricane Matthew in 2016 and require significant mental and emotional support. There will also need to be psychosocial support for front-line responders—both international and national. Most importantly, Haiti needs a strong foundation of spiritual support. As we all know, our spiritual strength navigates us to overcome. The loss of churches has become discouraging to so many. Rebuilding is also a key component within the Haitian society. Spiritual care is at the forefront.

Protection initiatives need to be set in place to safeguard the communities from the malicious violence that goes on, especially surrounding women and girls. Groups at risk of violent attacks include: the elderly, people living with disabilities, and orphaned children.

Ending child sex-trafficking through mentoring is a priority we take very seriously. These savage, mindless, and cruel acts against children are way more common in Haiti, than anyone could ever believe. Building self worth and strong minds will over power this kind of treatment. When children are educated, and given structure in their lives, they are less likely to be targeted.

As the predators of Haiti go after the meek minded, our intent is to equip these children with the tools they need to learn how to build strong boundaries. It also creates the responsibility of awareness; understanding who and what is healthy for them to be around. The foundation of mentoring also demonstrates the spirit of discernment. Knowing when to listen to that voice within, so you know when to exit a situation, before it even happens. It is that kind of infrastructure that protects children. It is a very big deal to us that mentoring still exists on the ground because it directly helps our efforts to build nations and keep children safe.

The Restavèks are unpaid child servants living and working away from home. In principle, parental placement of a restavèk child involves the handover of child rearing responsibility to another household in exchange for the child's unpaid domestic service. Restavèk placement is generally viewed as a long term arrangement that may last for several years.

The traditional expectation is that the "caretaker" household will cover the cost of sending the restavèk child to school. The Créole term restavèk literally means someone who lives with another ("reste avec" in French). In some cases, outside children are treated almost as if they were informally adopted, but often they are treated very badly, virtually as slaves. There is a tendency for male restavèks to originate from rural areas, whereas girls tend to come from urban areas.

As restavèk teens get older, they are commonly tossed to the street to fend for themselves and become victims of other types of abuse and social exclusion. According to a study by "The Lancet," the rate of sexual assault against female restaveks is almost four and a half times greater than that of girls who are not restavèks. Of the female restavèks, one in nineteen are sexually assaulted per year, compared with one in eighty four girls who are not restavèks. With our mentoring program, we hope to prevent these horrible things, by teaching our youth the principles that will help them believe in themselves, humbly create their lives, and impact their community.

According to different studies, child domestic workers in Haiti number between 170,000 and 230,000, which represents around ten percent of the child population aged between five and seventeen. About two-thirds of the child domestic-helpers are girls and they are mostly found in rural areas.

The exploitation of children in domestic service is compounded by economic hardship in Haiti, with many of the receiving families living in poverty themselves. Over half of the population lives below the $1-a-day poverty line, and seventy six per cent live on less than $2 a day. The UN Special Rapporteur on Contemporary Forms of Slavery, its Causes and Consequences, Gulnara Shahinian, expressed deep concern over the highly exploitative nature of the 'restavèk' system in Haiti, which she considers to be a modern form of slavery.

The restavèk system often deprives children of their family environment and violates their most basic rights. As well as subjecting them to multiple forms of abuse including economic exploitation, sexual violence, and corporal punishment.

Rebuilding will include underpinning for, wash houses, electrical systems, communication/wireless towers, transportation, businesses, homes, schools, health facilities, and churches. This will be ongoing for many years as there are still people homeless from the 2010 earthquake and 2016's Hurricane Matthew.

Livelihood restoration is also important and will remain a growing concern. Businesses were destroyed, including some of the hotels in tourist areas. Given the high levels of existing poverty, there will be a need for the development of new revenue-generating activities.

A thriving agriculture is the overall goal we seek to reach. The many resources of the country should be used for good; providing solutions for its peoples needs. **Agriculture dominates non-agricultural activities by its potential to reduce poverty,** whether the comparison is within or between countries. I truly believe that agricultural innovation and technology hold the key to poverty reduction in developing countries.

Access to technology will provide the children with an array of resources to learn current events around the world. They will gain cultural knowledge, vast communication from all walks of life, and a variety of computer skills. There are no towers for the internet to ignite this type of access. Knowledge is power, but right now the majority of Haitians lack access to quality education. We must change that.

Investment in local startups in the country is a brilliant way for the economy to grow. Instead of outsourcing to purchase supplies, groceries, and other amenities, buying from the locals would provide enrichment to the upbringing of the land. All of us can set a precedent for change if we truly want too.

Solar power is another form of renewable energy in Haiti. It has a lot of potential, due to the country's warm and tropical location. In rural areas that do not receive electricity, such as Haiti's south department, people depend on the energy produced from generators.

MY VISION FOR HAITI

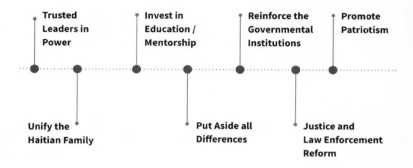

Trusted Leaders in Power

Invest in Education / Mentorship

Reinforce the Governmental Institutions

Promote Patriotism

Unify the Haitian Family

Put Aside all Differences

Justice and Law Enforcement Reform

I truly believe that the seeds we are planting in Haiti right now will grow into the future that I envision my children leading one day. I see my children as the paramount for the future generation, working hand in hand to continue the change we long so much to see. I see them supporting the Haitian youth, addressing challenges, and blossoming by providing a forum for the youth in the Caribbean.

I see my first born, Tevin, involved in the tech ecosystem. An adequate tech ecosystem will connect Haiti internationally. This will also help brand creators, set a new narrative for Haitian literacy around the world. We want Haiti to be tapped in globally. More connections means more jobs, more resources, improved cultivation, and a more stable foundation overall.

I see Kai designing the architecture for new and improved structures, buildings, homes, schools, shops, libraries, movie theaters, sporting fields for the children, and more. Kai will give the cosmetic foundation of Haiti a makeover, for the citizens and tourists.

I see my beautiful princess, Sidonie, educating the people on new principalities governing the rearing of Haitian people. I see her standing up for the rights of Haitian women, ensuring they are not ruled out when decisions are made for the country. I see her being an inspiration for young women and girls, helping them to rise above the trafficking their ancestors were forced to endure. I see my little Sidonie completely eradicating the corrupt treatment of young girls.

"The wolf shall dwell with the lamb, and the leopard shall lie down with the young goat, and the calf and the lion and the fattened calf together, *and a little child shall lead them.*"

– ISAIAH 11:6

There is no doubt in my mind that Haiti will rise up and once again, become the Pearl of the Caribbean islands that she used to be. I pray everyday that I will be there with my children and grandchildren, to see it all. **I truly believe that I was buried for hours, so that I could come out transformed into something greater. The rubble changed my life forever.**

A LOVE LETTER TO HAITI

I'm coming back for you . . . You may think I'm over there in the land of the free and that I won't come back. Anything I do and the decisions I've made is to help you rise from the rubble . . . I remember leaving you in March 2015 like it was yesterday, but my constant trips are the testimony of my true intentions to help you rise. No person, place, thing, or country can ever take your special place in my heart. You have so much good, beauty, life and precious gifts about you that your children have not yet been discovered and they are hiding because you have been neglected and abused by people with bad intentions.

Thanks **AYITI** *for raising me, for inspiring me to double my daily efforts wherever I am and in whatever I do. You have taught me true faith in God, my everyday life is based on what I can't see now but knowing that it can be accomplished. You have taught me to embrace every little thing because you didn't have too much to give but what you gave me was worth it all. I learned from you to never complain for what's being taken but to go create what was missing. Thanks for sustaining me. I hope you will never see yourself as unworthy of love, support and beauty just because you couldn't become what the world wanted you to be right now.*

I will continue to hold myself as a mirror to all the beautiful and wonderful things inside you that you forget to see. I know you're still buried under the rubble, rubble of impunity, rubble of corruption, rubble of your past, rubble of injustice but one thing I truly believe is that you will rise one day. It may take some time and maybe more time than we can imagine but you will rise above everything and become who you are created to be.

Mwen renmenw **Ayiti Cheri! Peyi Zansèt yo!**

ACKNOWLEDGMENTS

I APPRECIATE YOU TAKING THE TIME to purchase and read my book. I hope something that you've seen or felt with what I've shared, allows you to feel like you can continue to dream, even bigger. There is nothing that I've been able to do and achieve that you can't. I feel honored to have you taking your precious time to read my story and most importantly to support my work in my home country Haiti and Dominican Republic. I pray that each of you were able to learn something to empower you through my book, something to remind you of your potential. As a survivor from the earthquake in Haiti in 2010, I continue to take advantage of every moment, experience, and opportunity life gives me.

Throughout the book, my main focus is on the key principles and experiences that have helped me rise from my own rubble in life and invite everyone to rise from their own rubble. I believe that we all have the power, potential and capacity to become anything we want in this life.

Writing this book took a village, lots of work, desire, consistency and sweat. Sometimes I asked myself if I would ever get it done. This book represents so much more than the years it took to write. I owe a million thanks to those who believe in me and my mission since the beginning. Thanks to my grandparents from the other side, thanks to my mom, dad and my eternal wife who lovingly and enthusiastically cheered me on at every speaking engagement and those who never get tired of listening to my story as a survivor.

I'd like to echo every word from those who endorsed this book, to my parents, my amazing wife, my friends, my team and the loyal friends and supporters who have supported our work over the years, thank you so much! Mèsi anpil! Your support means everything as we all rise from our own rubble to be the maker of our own destiny.

Thank you! Mèsi! Gracias! Merci!

For any speaking engagements, visit
ariseprojects.org

ikoneklifecoaching.com

Or email support@ariseprojects.org

ABOUT THE AUTHOR

Williamson is a certified Life Coach for youth, adults, and emerging leaders, more specifically a Personal Growth and Success Coach. After two years of serving as a missionary in 2013-2015, Williamson discovered his interest in humanitarian work, specifically in the nonprofit world. Williamson founded his nonprofit organization back in 2016 that works in Haiti and the Caribbean **ARISE Project For Humanity.** He started his private coaching program called "**Ikonèk Life Coaching**". Ikonek connects teens, students, and emerging adults to their best purpose in life.

He is also invested in startup businesses within his hometown in Haiti. He has traveled far and wide to motivate young leaders to become victorious success stories and survivors, by showing and inspiring others through his love, faith, and his story as a survivor.

Learn more at **www.ariseprojects.org** or **www.ikoneklifecoaching.com**

Made in the USA
Middletown, DE
11 June 2022